For Louise, without whom none of this would ever have been possible.

For my girls Jess, Lon, Rach, I hope this inspires you to

Live a Life Worth Living.

For more information and inspiration go to:

www.the4pillarsoflife.com.au

www.facebook.com/the4pillarsoflife

No part of this book may be reproduced in any written, electronic, recording, or photocopying form without written permission of the author.

Cover Design: Lauren Rosel, Rubik Design
Interior Design: Lauren Rosel, Rubik Design
Formatting: The Hunting House
Publisher: Ingram Spark
ISBN: 978-0-6480893-0-8
© 2017 John Rosel. All rights reserved.

Table of Contents

The 4 Pillars of Life vii
What is this book all about? viii
Who is this Book aimed at? ix
What is Mind? x
What is Body? x
What is Soul? xi
What is living? xi
Who are you taking this journey for? xii
About the Author xii
How to get the most from this book xiv

MIND 1
Where's your head at? 4
Core Value Beliefs 18
Identifying Goals 28
Create an Action Plan 39
Day Dreaming & Living the Goal Now 44
The Myth of Control 46
Belief, Attitude, & Conscious Living 51
Fear…..Do you Really Understand it? 62
Motivation 77
Enjoy the Ride 86

Adjust your rudder 89
Remember why... 92

BODY 93

What is Old Boys Health & Fitness, and Why We Must Change? 96
Let's Take a Physical Inventory 101
The 4 Physical Pillars 111
The 'Menu' Approach to Health & Fitness 115
The Warm-Up 122
Strength and Conditioning 126
Stamina and Aerobic Fitness 130
Flexibility, Warm Down, Yoga 141
Nutrition, Diet and Supplements 145
Tracking and Measuring Progress 161
Motivation 171
Personal Health 175

SOUL 181

What is Soul? 186
The Subconscious Master 189
The Energy Circle 195
Loathing Life….or….Living Life 206
A Life's Purpose…..Don't worry if you don't have one ...212
The Warrior Code 221

The Middle Way 240
The Backyard Buddhist 243
Tools to Help You Achieve..246
Nurture V Nature..258
Opinions are Overrated..263
When the going gets tough…..Take smaller steps...........267

LIVING 271

Stocktake Time..274
Comfort Zone..278
A Sense of Adventure 282
Zen Living..285
The Intangibles..291
Stop Waiting for the Right Time 294
Travel Time..297
Work, Career, Passion..299
Time Management..305
Status Anxiety...313
Relationships...321
Food, Wine, Beer & Song...327

The 4 Pillars of Life

By

John Rosel

What is this book all about?

We all want to Live a Life Worth Living, live an adventurous life, and have a story to tell when we are older, but too many of us just 'get by'. We watch as other people seem happy and content, or are successful, and all we do is look for reasons why it doesn't work for us. We have regrets about the past, we worry about the future, and we just let the adventure of life slip by.

This book is a gathering of my own thoughts and experiences. It is not intended to be an unshakeable truth. It is however meant to open your mind to alternative ways of thinking and to create debate within yourself about how you can take control of your life and live it to the fullest.

This book is a journey of self-discovery through the maze of what makes a Life Worth Living. It is a guide to living a richer and fuller life, and a course of action to being a better man, in a world where the image and expectations of what a man should be, has been distorted beyond recognition, and beyond the achievement of the average *Old Boy*.

This book identifies the 4 Pillars of a great life–

1. Mind
2. Body
3. Soul
4. Living

Each of these 4 Pillars are dependent on each other and are intrinsically intertwined. While being independent areas of our life, they impact each other and create balance, or imbalance, throughout our life depending on our attitude and how we view the world at various stages of our lives.

The biggest issue we face is that we live our lives subconsciously. We have, through a life time of experiences, developed a set of beliefs and preconceived ideas, on which we automatically act and react to the world around us. We rarely think for ourselves and because of that we are often living someone else's goals and dreams and wonder why we feel so unfulfilled.

Who is this Book aimed at?

Whilst this book can be a valuable resource for anyone, you will notice a leaning towards what I refer to as *'Old Boys'*.

So who or what is an Old Boy?

Firstly it is not an age, it is a state of mind. The opposite of an Old Boy is an Old Man and there are Old Men who are 25 and Old Boys who are 70. An Old Boy is at that stage of his life when he starts to question what it's all about, he has a feeling that there is more to life but he just can't seem to work out what it is? An Old Man by comparison has thrown in the towel and doesn't try anymore, is happy with a mediocre life, and happy to tell everyone how good he once was.

Old Boys have a growing career, a growing family, growing responsibilities, and the carefree life of their youth seems a distant memory. But surely there must be more to life than this. It's an age when men are susceptible to depression and is a time when men can feel lost.

Old Boys tend to be a forgotten breed. Society dictates that men don't talk about personal issues and if they do they are seen as weak, and as such they just shut up and get on with it.

This book is an opportunity for Old Boys to have a look at themselves and their lives, in their own time and in their own way, and hopefully provides some guidance on those issues that affect all men, but that are never spoken about. It aims to allow us to take back control of our lives and live a life worth living.

What is Mind?

Mind is a reference to the way we think, our cognitive self, both conscious and subconscious. How have we been influenced to think the way we do? What impact does our thinking have on our lives? How our subconscious has the greatest impact on our lives, and we don't even know it. How modern media impacts how we see the world. What do we control in our lives? How do we stay motivated in tough times? Why is goal setting so hard? And why is it easier to stop trying and just go with the flow, rather than persevering? Why do we view the goal as more important than the journey?

What is Body?

As we grow older and 'life' starts to get in the way, our physical health can often take a back seat. The longer we lose focus on our physical health the harder it is to get back into shape, and when we try we train like we did in our youth and wonder why injuries and a lack of motivation are playing havoc with us.

This part of the book provides some concepts and guidelines, based on my own training experiences, that can help you not only get back into shape, but most importantly to maintain your physical health over the long term.

What is Soul?

Soul is often closely linked to Mind, but the difference for me is that Mind is mechanical for want of a better word. It is how the mind works, how we think, what impacts us, and how we can influence.

Soul is intangible. It is the meaning for existence. The reason we get up in the morning, and the reason we want to keep pushing forward when things aren't so good.

There are a million books on spirituality, and I've read a lot of them, but this is not one of them. But it does take a look at the 'Why' question in some detail, and offers some insights into my own philosophy as a **Backyard Buddhist**.

What is living?

Of the 4 Pillars, Living is the one that locks them all together. After all, this is what life is all about……to really live…...not just to exist like so many people do. This doesn't mean that by getting Mind, Body and Soul right that Living will fall into place. Living is its own Pillar and is perhaps the culmination or 'icing on the cake'. That doesn't mean you don't start Living until you have the other 3 Pillars perfect, in fact it is crucial you start living now to help bring the other 3 Pillars together. The 4 Pillars of Life are not mutually exclusive and one without the other creates disharmony.

Living in this context covers many things including –

- Comfort Zones
- A Sense of Adventure

- Travel
- Living in the Moment
- Career and Work
- Financial Status
- Status Anxiety
- Relationships
- Food, Wine, Beer and Song

Who are you taking this journey for?

Take a moment to think about who you are taking this journey of self-improvement for? Your wife, your kids, your friends?

There is only one person you are taking this Journey for….. **YOU.**

If you won't commit to self-improvement for yourself, you certainly won't be able to commit to do it for others. As the best coach the NRL has ever seen (Wayne Bennett) said once, "If you won't go out and play hard and tough to prove a point to yourself….you certainly won't do it for your team mates".

Improvement of the self leads to improvement of others. Be the change you want to see.

About the Author

I was born in 1969 and I'm 47 years old at the time of writing. This book has come about through the 40 odd years of experiences I've had while making my own way in the world. I had a

About the Author

fairly standard family life until I was 12 when I was sent away to boarding school, and I've been making it up as I go along ever since then. I've made an amazingly large amount of mistakes along the way because I was never one to ask for help or guidance and I prided myself on being independent, until at a point in my life I started to realise there were other ways of doing things, and just maybe, I wasn't always right and everyone else wasn't always wrong.

After I left boarding school I worked in the finance industry for 10 years before entering the property development industry where I still am today. I had 10 years with a major national property developer, trying desperately to climb the corporate ladder, before I struck out on my own and started my own Project Management Company. That was 13 years ago and I am still working for myself today. Whilst the last few years of the Global Financial Crisis have been difficult for all of us, the personal growth that the hard times have given me is beyond worth, and is a major contributor to the thoughts and guidelines in this book.

Sport has always been a big part of my life and I have been involved in Athletics, Gymnastics, Rugby League and Martial Arts for most of my life. I hold 3 Martial Arts Black Belts including a 4th Degree in BJC Muay Thai, a 1st Degree in Tae Kwon Do, and a Black Belt in Zen Do Kai Karate, and I run a club called *'Old Boys Thai Boxing'*.

I am blessed with a beautiful wife and 3 beautiful daughters (no sons, I think someone upstairs has a lousy sense of humour). My life hasn't been extraordinary but I have also had some experiences that few people have, and for some reason I feel the need to share my thoughts on life, and of taking back control of your life. I really hope that this book gets you to question your life, where you are, and opens your eyes to the possibilities of living a life worth living.

How to get the most from this book

This book is structured into the 4 Pillars of Mind, Body, Soul and Living. Each of the Pillars are then broken down into a 12 step journey. Each step explores another aspect of that Pillar, an aspect that impacts our life on a daily basis. Many of the steps have suggested tasks and actions that you may want to try, to assist you on your journey of self-discovery.

The book is meant to be a journey and each step builds on the last. You don't need to work through in the order of Mind, Body, Soul, Living, and in fact start at whichever Pillar you want to work on first, but treat the whole book as a package. Remember the 4 Pillars work together to build a great life.

I really hope this book gives you even just one thing that sparks a difference in your life, and that your journey is great one.

John Rosel

www.the4pillarsoflife.com.au

MIND

Dusty Dreams

The steps are rotten,
The porch is tilted,
At dangerous angles,
The plants are wilted.

A front door hangs,
By a single hinge,
Inside I step,
And feel the twinge,

Of pain and loss,
Dreams turned to dust.
The mantelpiece above the fire,
Memories….hopes….lust.

In the shadows a man,
Old and frail,
Sits and ponders,
Why life has failed.

I can't see his face,
The shadows are dark.
Drift a little closer,
In recognition a spark,

Of fear and loathing,
I know this man,
From the shape of his face,
To the lines on his hands.
It's a mirror of time,
That lurks inside,

MIND

What I become,
If time decides.

I reel in shock,
My mind is spinning,
The room and its memories,
At once beginning,

To lose their shape,
The house is fading,
Away from vision,
Turn from hating.

* * *

And all at once,
I'm a child again,
On the lawn of my parents,
And for a second I can,

Remember a dream,
Of an old man lost,
Fading from memory,
Fading……….lost.

JR

MIND
The First Step on the Journey....

Where's your head at?

They say the start of any journey begins with the first step…..well I don't agree. The start of any Journey begins with lifting your head up above the crowd and having a good look at where you are. If you don't know where you are, how can you get to where you want to be?

We need to stop and take some time out from our everyday lives. We all live on auto-pilot 90% of the time and this is a major stumbling block to living a life we can be proud of. We don't think for ourselves. We don't stop to smell the roses.

But I think for myself, I hear you say! I am my own person! Really….? Every day you do the same thing as you did yesterday because you accept that this is what you do and you can't change the circumstances of your life. Everyday your thinking and attitudes are influenced by what you read in the newspapers and magazines, what you see on television, and what your friends and colleagues opinions are for that particular day. Even when you disagree with someone and have an opinion, are you really thinking for yourself, or are you justifying a stance that subconsciously makes you feel superior to that person?

> *The Journey starts when you lift your head above the crowd and ask "Where the hell am I?"*

Having an opinion is NOT thinking for yourself. The more you think for yourself, the more you realise the world is a complex and unpredictable environment, and that there is rarely any black and white, rather the world is shades of grey. This does not mean having an opinion is wrong, but the more you think for yourself and see people and circumstances from another's perspective, the less vigorously you hold onto fixed opinions…..and when you are confident enough in yourself, to have less fear about being 'right', this is a truly enlightening moment.

When doing any self-evaluating exercise, always start with the negatives first and finish on the positives. It's a small thing but has a big psychological effect. It's the same reason athletes always want to finish a training session with a good effort or with a good technical movement. Don't leave any situation in life on a negative if it can be helped.

So first up we need to brainstorm. I recommend buying an A4 notebook and a pen and keep this notebook specifically for this journey. I am a big believer in handwriting when working through a self-analysis process. It is slower and helps you think better. It is also more personal and provides a clearer picture in your mind's eye. It allows you to take the guides from this book and put things in your own words, which is clearer for you to comprehend. If you only have access to a computer then it's ok to write notes in digital format, but a special note book, handwritten, will produce the best results by far.

Whatever you do though, DO NOT read without taking notes……..It is so important in this process to write and put things in your own terms. What is read is quickly forgotten. What is written down has a significantly higher potential to be retained cognitively.

The Self-Analysis Process

It's important to do this exercise (and all the exercises throughout this journey) in a place where you won't be disturbed, with enough time that you don't feel pressured or your attention is focused on something else. Leave the mobile phone somewhere you can't reach it and turn off the sound. If you want the best results, then you have to focus your attention, which means limiting outside interference.

So with your notebook and pen at hand, a coffee/beer/wine (or beverage of choice), and seated in your 'Happy/Not to be Disturbed' place…..let's begin.

Clearing the Mind

At the commencement of each session, I like to run through a quick breathing exercise that helps relax the body and clear the mind. It's a simple process and is something many athletes and fighters use before competition.

Our world in this age is so interconnected. We are always in touch with friends, and the world, through social media. Through email and text our work lives have blurred the traditional 9 to 5 lines so much it's barely visible anymore. Technology is changing far more rapidly than we as humans are evolving, and as such the importance of mental 'time out', or being able to slow the pace in the mind, is becoming paramount to our mental health.

This simple process is not the solution, but it is a technique that can be used before any event, important meeting, commitment that is making you nervous, or at any time during the day when you need to clear the mind and refocus. It is also an excellent tool for the aftermath of a bad meeting, a bad day, or

a confrontation that has left you angry or frustrated.

'Old Boys' who haven't done this sort of thing before tend to have a feeling of "This is stupid"…."God I hope no one sees me"….."What is this New Age crap?"

Firstly this is a key reason to find a place you won't be disturbed. A place you won't be 'found out' as if you're doing something bad.

Secondly…Why do you give a crap about what others are thinking? Are you taking this journey for them or for you?

There are 3 keys –

1. Circular breathing
2. Focus points
3. The breath

A lot of books say you need to be seated in the Lotus position, or on your knees (*Seiza* in Martial Arts terminology), or have the hands folded into a certain position………I don't care what position you're in, it's all about the mind not about how the body is positioned. Besides how many 'Old Boys' can get into the Lotus position? If you do, make sure you have the Ambulance on speed-dial!

The only caution I would suggest is don't lie down flat. This tends to induce a feeling of sleep and that's not really what we are after. Seated in a chair, sitting on the ground, leaning against a tree….it doesn't matter. Just make it comfortable.

So you are now in a comfortable position. Just for the next 3-4 breaths focus your mind on the breath. Feel it entering into your nose, the cool air on the way in and the warm air on the way out. Now close your eyes and take your first circular breath.

To circular breathe, breathe in through the nose and imagine the air is a white light. It passes through your nose and then travels down your spine. As it travels down the spine actually imagine you can feel it lighting the spine up as it moves down. At the bottom of the spine the air/light enters your Dan Tian which is the area between the navel and the groin. In Martial Arts and eastern practices this is considered the centre of the body.

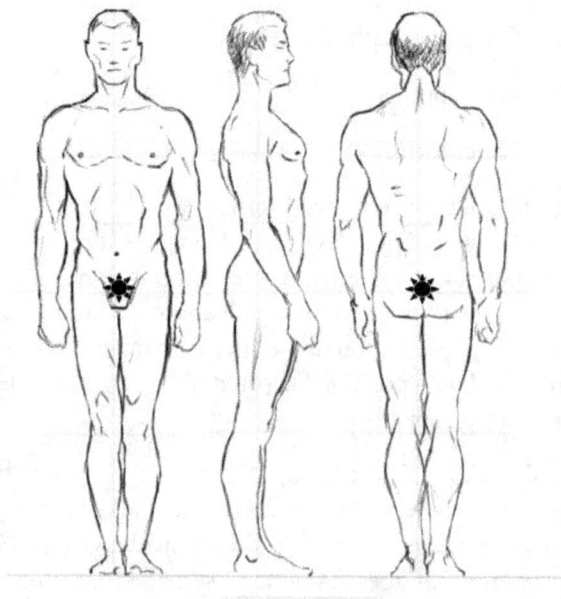

✹   **Dan Tian**

As the air enters the Dan Tian it begins to fill the area with an expanding light until the lungs are full. Then you start to breathe out through the mouth.

The next step is a tricky part to get used to, but just try. Imagine the breath leaving the mouth is black smoke, all the toxins, and negativity, that is stored in your body, leaving the body. At the same time the light in the Dan Tian expands into all parts of the body to replace this 'black smoke'.

Once you have taken one 'Circular Breath' you may find in the first few times you do this that you are puffing a little. This is because by focusing on breathing into the Dan Tian, it is making you breathe to the bottom of your lungs. This is something we rarely do as we tend to breathe shallow and don't use the full capacity of our lungs. After the first circular breath just breathe normally again for a few breaths, and then when you are ready, do another circular breath.

Do this for 3 circular breaths, then on the exhale of the last one, open your eyes and start to work on the first thought exercise below.

If this seems all a little weird and 'New Age'……...just man up and try something different. Part of your reluctance to try something a little different, is a symptom of the rut we get caught in in our lives. There is no right or wrong way to do this, this is just the way I do it. Don't get frustrated as your mind continues to wander, just refocus back on your breathing.

The Analysis

The first part of this analysis is to work through each of the questions below that look to focus on elements and situations in your life that affect the way you think, and hence the way your mind is wired.

As you write down each issue that comes to mind, I want you to also write down how that issue makes you feel. Don't think too much, just write down how you feel immediately. I suggest setting out your notebook something like the following –

Self Analysis
The First Step in the Journey

What Troubles You?		
Situation/Thing/Person	Feelings/Emotions/Thoughts	Root Causes

What affects the way you think everyday?		
Situation/Thing/Person	Feelings/Emotions/Thoughts	Root Causes

The first two columns are what we are looking at in this stage. Identify the situation/thing/person, and then identify immediate feelings/emotions/thoughts that come up.

We will work through the 'Root Cause' column once our initial brainstorming is complete.

- **What troubles you?**

We all have issues that we think about constantly. Issues that keep us awake at nights worrying about what might happen. Brainstorm and identify these issues. Don't think about why, or look for solutions, just write them down and move forward. There will be issues that come to mind but you may dismiss them as silly or you should be stronger.......STOP....Just write them all down. This is a brainstorm session, and review and editing is a separate process. Just get it all out of your head and down onto paper.

- **What affects the way you think every day?**

What does your day to day routine consist of? Think about what you do every minute of the day? What takes your attention and focus? Think about your circle of friends. How do they think and how do you feel about them? Think about your circle of acquaintances and work colleges. How do they make you feel?

- **What gets you angry?**

What really gets under your skin? What issues cause you to form a very strong opinion one way or the other? Initially write down what first comes to mind in terms of the reasons you get angry. Don't analyse too deeply, we'll get to that.

- **What frustrates you?**

What frustrates you? What can you see can be done better? Who do you see that could be doing better?

Many of these topics overlap, but that's ok, just brainstorm in the first instance, get it all down on paper.

- **What are your weaknesses?**

Now don't beat yourself up with this part of the exercise. Try and be as detached as possible and identify areas you are weak in. It could be communicating with new people, you may get angry easily, you may get frustrated easily, you may put yourself down regularly, just think about situations in your life you wish you could address better.

- **Who are your circle of friends and acquaintances?**

Now identify 3 circles of influence as follows –

Inner Circle - People you love. Relatives. Close Friends. People you see every day.

Mid-Circle – Your acquaintances. People you know and see regularly. Work colleges.

Outer Circle – People you don't necessarily know but who you see or watch regularly and who influence the way you think. It can be negative or positive influence. Do you follow politics? Who? Do you follow sport? Who?

The Positives

….and now for the positives. This can be a difficult process for many people. Certainly it's harder than acknowledging our negatives because it's in our nature to focus on negatives and not positives. 'Old Boys' often find this especially difficult as we are programmed not to 'big note' ourselves, or talk about any of our strengths. Not being able to focus on strengths is one of the major problems with people's lives.

You may want to end the session with the negatives, and look to regroup and do the positives session separately. This can be helpful especially if you are feeling stuck on the positives. A fresh start tomorrow can be helpful.

As with the negatives, try not to apply judgement to yourself. Try to look at yourself as a separate being and look at recognising your strengths as elements of the whole you. Don't fall into the trap of writing down a strength and then judging and thinking that you really don't qualify for that strength. Just brainstorm without judgement.

What do you enjoy?

What makes you happy? What do you enjoy doing? Who do you enjoy spending time with? Who or what makes you laugh?

What are your strengths?

What are you ok at? What makes you feel like you have achieved something? What would your friends say is good about you, or what do they think you do well?

Root Causes

Well done on completing this brainstorming session. Don't think that it has to be 100% correct or that you can't go back to various sections as you progress and write further things down. As you start to analyse, other things will crop up and get you thinking in a new direction, this is what we want so if that happens, stop, go back and record, and come back again.

Now that you have the brainstorm session complete its time to go back and look more deeply at each of the items in your list and start to look deeper at what I call the Root Causes.

This process requires looking beyond the surface emotion or feeling that is felt in a particular situation and look to what is really happening. At their absolute core, negative emotions generally revolve around the Fight or Flight instinct, or the Survival Instinct.

Let me give you some examples from my own life and from an exercise I did some 10 years ago, that may help to explain what to look for.

What troubles you?

- **Situation/Thing/Person**
  - I don't handle conflict well in the workplace. Even to the point where a simple negotiation becomes a conflict in my mind.

- **Feelings/Thoughts/Emotions**
  - I feel I am being attacked personally
  - I feel anger and aggression

- **Root Cause**
  - As a child I was bullied badly. I often felt embarrassed and humiliated. That led to a deep fear of confrontation.
  - However I started to learn to fight back and I found even if I was beaten up I felt better about having stood up for myself.

- This cycle of bullying, embarrassment turning to anger, to fighting, became engrained in me when I was at a vulnerable age.
- I left home when I was 12 so lacked a strong guiding male role model
- As such I had become so highly sensitive to people disagreeing with me that my mind assumes this is an attack on my person and my best course of response is to attack before I get embarrassed or hurt.
- Fear of being embarrassed
- Linking aggression (verbal not just physical) as the solution
- Lack of confidence in my own self
- Viewing the other person as attacking me personally, and not recognising, or trying to understand their position to see if we can work with them.

So from this analysis I have looked past the face value emotion that the other person is a dick and they are just trying to ruin my career. I have identified the core emotions of embarrassment and fear, which then comes from a lack of confidence in my own ability.

What troubles you?

o **Situation/Thing/Person**
- I trust people too quickly and then feel let down easily.

- **Feelings/Thoughts/Emotions**
  - I want to build relationships with like-minded people so my life is easier
  - When I'm let down I feel anger
- **Root Cause**
  - This is again a cause of my earlier years of bullying and fighting
  - I try and trust people and form friendly relationships quickly because I am trying to avoid the conflict.
  - However I see the first sign of disagreement as conflict and move from friendly to aggressive very quickly.
  - It's a protection mechanism. Protecting myself from hurt and embarrassment

So from this analysis I see that even my trying to be friendly and trusting is a protection mechanism.

Now work your way through each of your issues and take time to analyse each. Don't fall into the trap of laying blame, "It was my father's fault…" or "If that hadn't happened….". Try to identify reasons but do not attribute blame.

At this stage it is enough to recognise and acknowledge what the root cause really is. You may also notice throughout the analysis that the same few Root Causes start to appear. This is the 80/20 rule cognitively in play. 20% of our subconscious Root Causes create 80% of our conscious problems. The key is to be able to shine a light into the unconscious and recognise what is really happening, and recognise the face value emotions as symptoms, not causes.

Don't look for solutions at this stage as that is to come in the next steps on the journey.

MIND
The Second Step on the Journey......

Core Value Beliefs

Values are things, that when we understand them, become conscious of them, and live by them, create a life of peace and fulfilment, even in the toughest of times. In old Samurai culture they are called the Virtues of Bushido, in the romanticism of Medieval Knights it was referred to as the rules of Chivalry, its referred to in many other societies as the Warrior Code, often in modern society it is called 'being true to yourself', and I refer to it as 'Living with Honour'.

Values are your core beliefs. The heart of who you are as a person. When you are at a crossroads in your life and an important decision has to be made, there are two avenues to assess a decision by –

1. Cognitively and Factually – Assessing a situation based on facts, based on an assessment of the positives and negatives, using tangible outcomes on which to base a decision, the things that bring short term happiness.

2. Core Value Beliefs – Making a decision based on your core beliefs, the things that ultimately bring long term peace and fulfilment to your life.

Both Cognitive Facts and Core Values are important in critical decision making, and one should not be utilised at the expense of another, however when you have analysed all the elements of an issue, your final decision should be in alignment with your Core Values. You can guarantee that any direction you take in life that is not in alignment with your core values, will be a short term solution only, a dead end track off the main pathway of life. It may lead to short term happiness and tangible results, but it will not be sustainable in terms of long term fulfilment.

When we are younger we often make decisions based on short term gain, and at a younger age we tend to push through with the view that a greater good lies down the track. But we soon come to realise that the greater good always comes back to our Core Values and Beliefs, and that all we end up doing is taking a detour of self-discovery. As 'Old Boys' we have taken many detours in our life and we are at a different stage of self-realisation, where the importance of longer term fulfilment and peace are more important than short term gains. The classic Young Bull…Old Bull story.

Values and Core Beliefs are intangible in nature but very tangible in action. In broad terms Core Value Beliefs can be split into 6 categories as follows. These categories overlap each other and are often entwined, so don't treat them as separate entities that each have right or wrong answers. They are abstract by nature and you may see two or three key Core Beliefs shine through in each category.

The following list of Core Beliefs is followed by some example questions to ask yourself that will help you isolate the various elements of your life and what Core Beliefs may lie behind decisions you make.

- **Personal Identity** – How do you see yourself? What do you like about yourself? How do you want others to see you? How do you want to be remembered when you die? What is your 'work'? What do you do?

- **Achievement** – What is my sense of purpose? What is my legacy? What 'mark' do I want to leave on the world? What is the intangible reason, feeling, or emotion, I have for the goals I am chasing?

- **Relationships** – What kind of friend do I want to be? What kind of Work College do I want to be? What kind of husband do I want to be? What kind of father do I want to be?

- **Creativity** – What do I day dream about? If I achieved my day dreams, how would that make me feel? What do I do that makes me laugh? How do I express myself when I feel like no one is watching?

- **Contribution and Compassion** – What would you do for others with no expectation of return? What inspires you to do this? Who are you inspired to help?

- **Search for Meaning** – If your life had one purpose, what would it be? What does searching for a deeper meaning in your life, mean to you?

A word on Destructive Beliefs. As Old Boys some of us will have entrenched belief systems that we will never succeed, our life has not worked out as we wanted to, everything I touch turns out badly, I drink too much, I smoke too much etc.

These destructive beliefs have been built up over a lifetime of experiences. They are NOT core beliefs. You may work through this exercise and struggle to come up with any answers to the core beliefs, if that happens for you in one or more of the areas then just day dream. If nothing was stopping you, what kind of person would you want to be in each of these core belief areas.

Be very conscious of negativity creeping in when you do this. You may say for Achievement that you want to be someone who creates a new product that helps others, but you immediately think "That's stupid, I will never be smart enough, or have enough money, or be confident enough". STOP......that is a protection mechanism. Just day dream and put down a positive answer......whether you think it is achievable or not.

An example list of some responses to the Core Value Belief questions above are as follows. This is far from an exhaustive list and is only meant to start you thinking in a direction.

- Personal Identity
    - Someone who gets things done
    - A leader
    - Someone who carries out instructions well
    - A good worker
    - Enjoy the battle of business
    - A strong leader
    - A compassionate person
    - Quiet and compassionate
- Achievement
    - I want to be self-sufficient in life
    - I feel I am destined for something better
    - I want to be remembered as a nice person

> *"Keep looking below surface appearances. Don't shrink from doing so just because you might not like what you find".* **General Colin Powell**

- I want to help others achieve their health goals
- Success in business is important to me as it makes me feel I am capable
- Relationships
  - I want to be a friend that others can come to for advice
  - I want to be a leader in my career
  - I feel good when I complete tasks and get praise from my boss
  - I want my children to see me as someone they can talk to about anything
  - My wife is my best friend
- Creativity
  - I dream about being my own boss
  - I feel good when I am working hard to deliver a project
  - I feel good when I create a new concept
  - I like to inspire people with my out of the box thinking
  - I like to play guitar
  - I like to draw
- Contribution and Compassion
  - I feel good when I help someone with a personal problem

- I feel good when I help a college work through a big workload
- I feel good when I help a homeless person
- I feel good when I motivate someone to improve their health
- Search for Meaning
  - I want to feel at peace and be happy with what I have
  - It's important to me to always look to improve the kind of person I am
  - I like to 'go with the flow' and let life unfold

TASK:

Time for action….

So with this guide at hand, go back to your happy/not to be disturbed place, and lets start thinking about all this. Remember to start with the breathing and focusing exercise and then just brainstorm into your notebook, without judgement or too much thought. Just get it all out of our head and onto paper.

Outcomes

So how did you go? Remember you may not accomplish all this in one sitting. Don't put time limits on yourself, but also make sure you are not brainstorming and then starting to analyse what you have written. The first step is always a 'thought download' and then the next step is to go back and start to analyse.

You may find that some of the six Core Belief Value areas do not resonate as strongly with you as others. You may struggle to come up with many thoughts in some areas and be overwhelmed with thoughts in other areas. This is good. We are all different and what this is showing you is where your strengths lie and ultimately what drives you. For example I am not that engaged by the Contribution and Compassion area. This is not to say I am not compassionate, but that my strengths lie in other areas such as creativity, and through creativity I am able to contribute…and maybe even show some compassion.

The aim now is to identify some themes from your brainstorming, in each of the 6 Core Belief areas, and then structure them into a core belief word or statement. Many texts on this process will ask you to analyse down to a single word, but my belief is that is a limiting process and may not adequately explain the feeling or emotion. Having said that, don't make it War and Peace. Get it down to a single one line sentence that answers what and why? What is the emotion or belief that resonates with me, and why does it resonate with me?

Be careful of the Why question. The answer to 'Why' should be an intangible emotion, not a tangible answer such as, I like being rich, or I like having a big car. What you are looking for is the feeling that being rich or having a big car gives you.

Following are some examples of different summaries that others have come up with in the past. This may assist in working through your own list. Remember get it down to a single sentence that answers what and why.

Personal Identity

- I am a leader as it makes me feel confident and respected

- I help people with problems as it makes me feel happy

- I help people less fortunate than me as it makes me feel at peace

- I want to motivate others to be better people as that makes me a better person
- I am an honest person and treat others with respect

Relationships

- I like it when friends come to me for advice. It makes me feel like I am contributing to improving their lives
- I enjoy being a leader at work and in my career as I enjoy seeing a project come to life
- I want to be a friend and father to my children so they can have the best life
- I want to be a friend who can be relied on as friendship is important to me
- I am honest in my business dealings as Integrity is important to me

Achievement

- I want to work for myself as I enjoy being in control of my own decisions
- I help others achieve their goals and this makes me feel I have contributed to the world
- I want to be a leader in business as I feel I can make a difference there

Creativity

- I like creating new ideas as I enjoy the excitement of creating something new

- I enjoy playing music as it makes me feel at ease and relaxed
- I enjoy creating works of art and the joy it brings to others makes me happy
- I want to be my own boss as I want to be creative without restrictions of others

Contribution and Compassion

- I enjoy helping those less fortunate as it makes me feel I am a good person
- I like being a leader who can make people's lives better as I really feel I can contribute
- I treat everyone with compassion as it makes me feel at peace

Search for Meaning

- Being at peace without anxiety and worry is most important to me
- Improving each day, even in the smallest step, makes me feel content

The examples above cover a range of personality types. Your aim is to identify 2 or 3 key values that can describe your core beliefs in a What and Why sentence. You will know when you have identified the real source of your core beliefs as the What and Why will resonate with you at the deepest level.

Over time, as life and the circumstances that make up your life change, your core beliefs and values may change. Don't ever be afraid to go back and alter the statement or add new and fresh ideas. This is part of your personal growth and things are meant to change.

So…..finalise your Core Value Belief statements now and keep them handy for use throughout this journey and when making decisions on anything in life from here on in.

MIND
The Third Step on the Journey......

Identifying Goals

There are so many books, so many courses, and so much literature on Goal Setting you could spend a lifetime reading and researching and never even make a dent in it. So here I go adding my 2 bobs worth to it!

Humans by nature are materialistic and as such so much goal setting focuses on materialistic gain, which in itself is ok, but if you don't get to the core of the feelings and emotions the materialist achievement will give you, then you will never be able to maintain motivation, and if you do reach the goal it will quickly loose its lustre and you will realise you are still unfulfilled. Nothing I will espouse below is new, buts it's my way, which has changed as I've grown into an 'Old Boy'.

A good example of setting a material goal without the associated deeper Core Value emotions and feelings, is through my years of Martial Arts experience. Anyone who starts martial arts has a goal to become a Black Belt, and rightly so as that is a great achievement. Over the years I would say 90% of people I have seen achieve their Black Belt, turn up to training for the next month proudly sporting their Black Belt, but then they slowly drift away and you rarely see them again. Why? Because the goal has been getting a particular coloured belt. For others they truly believe that at Black Belt they will start to learn the inner secrets like the Five Finger Death Punch or other amazingly fictitious techniques. What happens is they start to realise they are the same person the day after their

Black Belt, as they were the day before.

A phrase you will hear often from Martial Arts instructors is…."The Journey begins when you get your Black Belt". Wonderful sentiments, but no one ever explains to the student what that means, often because the instructor doesn't know, because that's what their instructor said to them so they just regurgitate wonderful platitudes as it makes them feel windswept and mysterious.

The core to successful goal setting, and especially for 'Old Boys' at this mid-life stage, is understanding the feelings and emotions that achieving a tangible goal, will bring you. That is what brings deep satisfaction, and long lasting happiness.

Life Mapping

Life Mapping is a combination of two recognised strategies called Mind Mapping and Goal Storming.

> *The meaning of life is not simply to exist, to survive…..but to move ahead, to go up, to achieve, to conquer.* Arnold Schwarzenegger

Mind Mapping is an abstract approach that uses pictures, diagrams, doodles and drawings to effectively "Map Out" a path for your life. This method is very useful for those who are creatively or visually inclined and gives a level of creative clarity to the vision for your life.

Goal Storming is a more methodical approach using topics or areas of your life, lists, and written brain storming. This method is suitable for those who are more 'right brained' and methodical in their approach to assessing things.

My approach does not dictate that either way is better, in fact I believe if you are a methodical thinker that a level of creative analysis can often open you up to areas of thinking you have not experienced and hence may open new neural pathways that create new and unique thinking, and of course vice versa for those who are creative try creating some lists and analysis by detailed exploration of ideas. In other words adjust this process to work for you as an individual, but pushing your thinking outside your normal day to day methods is encouraged as you will be surprised by what this produces.

Goal Setting Steps

In this process of setting Goals, there are 4 clear steps. This approach is what I call Reverse Engineering as it takes a look at where you want to be at the end of your life, then works backwards. My 4 steps are –

1. Compartmentalise
2. Looking Back
3. Core Belief Filter
4. Equating the Gap

1. **Compartmentalise**

When setting goals you need to compartmentalise your life so that you can focus on a particular part of your life and the emotions and thoughts that go with that component. If you think too broadly you will be unable to get to the essence of what you really want, and you will be stuck with tangible goals that are not linked to your Core Value Beliefs.

There are the 4 main areas of life that are the inherent basis of this approach, being Mind, Body, Soul, and Living. For the purpose of goal setting these can be broken down as follows –

1. Mind
   a. Personal Growth
   b. Educational Achievements
2. Body
   a. Physical Health
   b. Physical Activities and Achievements
3. Soul
   a. Spiritual Growth
   b. Relationships
4. Living
   a. Financial Achievement
   b. Career/Business Achievement
   c. Travel and Adventure

2. **Looking Back**

Now let's look into each of these life elements separately, and work through each of the following questions and examine your thoughts. I recommend working through each element to the completion of this process, then going back and starting the process again for the next element. This helps maintain a train of thought and keeps you focused on that particular area of your life.

Brainstorm

Visualise that it's your 100th birthday and you're sitting alone contemplating your life and answer the following questions in that frame of mind. Understand that I want you to look at your life on completion looking backwards over a lifetime of experiences, achievements, failures, and everything in between. Visualise how you want your life to have been?

Mind – Personal Growth and Educational Achievements

- o What level of education have I achieved?
- o What did I do to better my knowledge?
- o What did I do to become a better person?
- o What did I do with the cards I was dealt?
- o What took me out of my comfort zone?
- o What kind of person do people say I am?
- o What kind of person do I think I am?

Body – Physical Health

- o How did I treat my body? (Did I make my 100th or has poor living cost me dearly?)
- o What was I like when I was at my peak physical shape?

Body – Physical Activities and Achievements

- o What sport did I play?
- o What did I achieve?

Identifying Goals

- o What did I do to keep fit and challenge myself?

Soul – Spiritual Growth

- o What kind of person am I? Compassionate? Angry? Tolerant? Bigoted?
- o Who have I helped?
- o Who has helped me?
- o Whose lives have I made a difference to?
- o What did I do to improve my spiritual growth?

Soul – Relationships

- o What kind of husband have I been?
- o What kind of father have I been?
- o What kind of Friend have I been?
- o What do people say about me?
- o Who is important to me?

Living – Financial Achievement

- o What have I achieved financially?
- o How did I achieve that?
- o Did I help others achieve their financial goals?

Living – Career/Business Achievement

- o What have I achieved in Business?

- What did I achieve in my career?
- Who have I influenced?
- Who has influenced me?

Living – Travel and Adventure

- Where have I travelled?
- What adventures have I had?

From this process you may find you have some negative thoughts and feelings, that's ok, make sure you write them all down. I don't subscribe to the school of thought that everything you say must be said or written in positive tones. Don't get me wrong, you must ultimately be a positive thinker but when self-analysing, negative thoughts and emotions help identify areas of our life we'd like to change, and are as useful as positive thoughts in this process.

Positive Conversion

From your brainstorm list, now summarise and dot point all your positive outcomes. Then take all your negative thoughts and turn them around into positive outcomes. Now you will be starting to get a feel for the type of person you want to be remembered as, the things you want to achieve, and the legacy you want to leave from your life.

Focus

From this positive conversion list I want you to now highlight your top outcomes and turn those outcomes into a tangible achievement. Keep the maximum number of outcomes to 3 to avoid becoming too generalised and to keep your focus sharp.

If you have more than 3 outcomes you may find that some items overlap and as such combine these into a more consolidated outcome. If you are struggling to get 3 outcomes you may be limited by your current circumstances. It's important you let this be a 'no holds barred' brainstorm. Some outcomes will seem unrealistic and unachievable….don't worry about that, just write them down without judgement or thought as to how on earth you could achieve them.

Turning the outcome into a tangible achievement is a critical step in the goal setting process. What we have tried to achieve with this process is identifying the thoughts and emotions that we want to achieve, but then identifying tangible achievements, actions, or behaviours that we can adopt that will lead us to that ultimate goal.

3. Core Value Filter

Remember the central theme of this process is to identify goals that correlate to our Core Values and Beliefs. Without a direct link to our Core Values, goals are merely dreams, and like waking from a dream and the dream starts to fade from memory, so too will your goals quickly lose momentum when you are not aiming for an emotion or outcome that is rooted in your Core Value Beliefs.

So with your top 3 outcomes now go back to the Second Step on our Journey where you identified your Core Value Belief System (you are writing this all down in your own personal Journal aren't you??)

Read each of your top 3 outcomes and review where that fits into your Core Beliefs and specifically what Core Belief does it reflect? Write the relevant core belief next to the relevant outcome.

If there is a disconnect between your Focused Tangible Achievement and your Core value Belief system, then review the Outcome and ask yourself the following question –

1. What is the emotion, feeling or behaviour that this outcome will bring me?

2. What did I do with this achievement to help others?

You must be able to answer these questions for any tangible outcomes for them to have meaning and to be a sustainable and achievable outcome. Adjust the wording of your outcome to meet your core values.

4. Equating The Gap

Now that you have established your Top 3 Outcomes, and confirmed they are in accordance with your Core Values, it's time to 'Equate the Gap'. This is the process of establishing where you are now, and where you want to be, and what is required physically, mentally, and emotionally to bridge that gap.

Don't start over-thinking or stressing about how you will bridge the gap, just understand what that gap is and the key attributes and actions that it will take to get there. For example one of your key outcomes may be to work for yourself. Currently you may work for an employer and as such the key attributes and actions that you may identify to close the gap may be as follows –

o Research and understand the market you want to go into

o Put a business plan together so you understand the financial commitment

- o Take some extra courses or form of study in a particular area
- o It will take a change of time commitment

Now you have the key attributes and actions that are required to close the gap. In this process you have taken a huge leap forward in understanding your life and where you want to be. At this stage that is all you need, the next step on this journey will deal with Action Plans and how to start taking consistent and achievable action towards tangibly closing the gap.

Bringing it all together

The following is a summarised guide of the goal identification process that we have detailed here. Follow this guide and refer back to the detail as required. Remember this is a guide, not a strict rule book that needs to be followed, but the general analytical process is –

1. **Identify your Core Value Beliefs**

The second step on the journey seeks to have you identify the intangible values that drive you and you live your life by.

2. **Identify your goals**

    a. **Compartmentalise**
    Separate your life into various components or areas of influence so you can focus down onto specific aspects of your life

    b. **Looking Back**

       i. **Brainstorm**
       Now within each component of your life ask yourself the questions we have suggested and

brainstorm all outcomes both positive and negative

ii. Positive Conversion
From your brainstorm summarise all your positive outcomes and convert any negative outcomes into positive statements

iii. Focus
Now identify your top (maximum of 3) outcomes and convert those into a Tangible Achievement.

c. Core Value Filter

Now take each Focused Outcome and revert back to your Core Value Beliefs and identify which Core Value Beliefs the outcome resonates with to ensure your Focused Tangible Achievements are in alignment with your Core Value Belief system.

d. Equating the Gap

Now look at where you want to be in terms of your Focused Tangible Achievement and where you are now. Be realistic and, without judgement or fear, understand what the gap is between now and where you want to be.

MIND
The Fourth Step on the Journey......

Create an Action Plan

Now that we have identified our Core Value Beliefs, actualised some tangible goals that align with our Core Value Beliefs, and we have equated the Gap between where we are and where we want to be, it's now time to start creating an action plan to cover the gap.

The key to achieving goals is to continually break down the gap into smaller and smaller achievable steps. Let's take an example goal below –

GOAL – To be self-employed and run my own business

THE GAP – I am currently employed by a national company working 50 hours per week.

So firstly identify the big picture elements in the gap. In this example they could include –

- I don't even know what business I would go into
- I have no educational qualifications
- I have no experience
- I don't have sufficient capital to set up my own business
- I don't have the time

First things first…..notice how every statement is negative. This is exactly what will happen when you do this exercise.

Your established patterns of thinking will immediately look for all the reasons you can't achieve this goal. Now as I said previously, bringing out all the negatives is not a bad thing and should not be discouraged. What you must not do however is let the negatives then stop you from proceeding further.

It's also important to understand that this list is not the end of the elements required to cover the gap. It is just that this is all you know now given the knowledge you have. As you start to progress you will identify other issues that come into play. That is excellent and means you are progressing on the journey. When you identify these other elements, work through the same exercise on breaking down the element into achievable smaller tasks.

Now that you have identified all these issues, the first action is to convert the Gap Statements into an element devoid of positive or negative terms. Many people will tell you to convert these to an "I will…." statement, or an "I have…." Statement. There is nothing wrong with this but at this stage I prefer to leave emotion aside and just state the case. I would convert the statements above as follows –

- I need to identify what business I will go into
- I may need further educational requirements
- I may need to gain some experience
- I need to understand capital requirements and funding structures
- I will need to be efficient with my Time Management

Create an Action Plan

So let's now start breaking each Gap Statement down into small achievable steps or tasks. Once you have identified a set of tasks or actions, then go back and order them in terms of priority, remembering that some actions may be required to be completed before others can be achieved. This is about identifying a pathway to your goal.

Once you have ordered them in priority order now put dates against them by which you believe you can have achieved the action or at least some results towards that task.

A key issue that will arise for many, and can be a point where the negative emotions start to come out again, and where many dreams are crushed, is that you will be able to identify actions and tasks up to a certain point but then it gets difficult to set tangible tasks after that stage and that is because you simply do not have enough knowledge at this time. Understand that if you have set a task where by you can clearly see all tasks through to completion....probably means you haven't set a high enough goal and that you have simply been procrastinating in the past. It doesn't mean you don't go out and achieve it, but look further and live big. So when you realise you have set some tasks into the future but there is still a gap between where you will be and your goal, simply make that a review stage where, having achieved all the tasks you have set yourself, you will go back to the start of this process and reset you tasks and action, now of course based on the knowledge you have achieved, and from a much better place that is far closer to your goal.

This process may end up looking something like the following.

1st Gap Statement - I need to identify what business I will go into

Action/Task	Achieve Date
Sit down and brainstorm my Strengths, Weaknesses, Likes and Dislikes. Brainstorm what I would like to do if I couldn't fail or if money was not an obstacle.	30.9.16
Research business opportunities that align with my brainstorm outcomes	30.10.16
Select my top 3 options and complete detailed research on what qualifications, education, and capital I need.	30.12.16

2nd Gap Statement - I may need further educational requirements

Source the courses or educational requirements I need and register and start studying	28.2.17

3rd Gap Statement - I may need to gain some experience

Research where I can gain the required experience and commence getting that experience	28.2.17

4th Gap Statement – Capital requirements and funding structures

Research ways of raising capital, savings measures I can take, and sources of equity I can talk to about my plan	30.3.17
Create a Business Plan	30.4.17

Understand which funding source I will be
pursuing And create a plan to achieve in a
set time   30.5.17

5th Gap Statement – I will need to be efficient with my Time Management

Research Time Management methodologies   30.9.16

Create a Time Management Plan   30.10.16

Now that you have identified a set of tasks it's time to document it in a format that aligns with your personality. As we discussed at the start of the Goal Setting component, some people are left brain thinkers and others are right brain. Some respond better to pictures and diagrams and others respond better to formal lists. Either way the key here is to create a one page, A3 size, Vision Board of your plan. This is then placed up on the wall or someplace where you will see it every day and will remind you and empower you to keep moving forward.

Always remember that finishing last always beats didn't finish, which in turn always trumps didn't start.

This Vision of your goal is supported by all your documents, lists and research that you will build up, but it is this visual reminder every day that will keep you focused. This Vision Board can have pictures of your goal, images, or words that inspire you, it can be typed or hand drawn, very neat or rough and ready, it is up to you, but pick things that will remind you every day **WHY** you are doing this.

When in doubt always remember it's about the journey of life, and remember that finishing last always beats didn't finish, which always trumps didn't start.

MIND
The Fifth Step on the Journey......

Day Dreaming & Living the Goal Now

Visualization is the act of thinking and feeling our goals in the present. The key here is 'feeling' the goals. By actually feeling what it would be like to reach your goal starts to open up new doors. In the end it is not the tangibility of the goal that is important, it is the feelings we get from having or achieving that goal. This is what drives us.

So how do we visualise? It's not as hard as it sounds and in fact as kids we did it all the time, our teachers just called it Day Dreaming. Our teachers and parents also told us to stop day dreaming and as such it has been instilled into us that day dreaming is bad and a waste of time. What a shame we have lost such a valuable resource for positive living.

So pick one of your Goals that you analysed in step 3 and the associated Core Value Belief that goes with it, and find yourself a quiet place (remember you're not be disturbed/happy place?). Now take a moment to work through the Breathing and Focusing exercise from step 1. Once you are relaxed, bring your mind to the goal you want to achieve and imagine you have achieved it. What is your life like? What is your day to day routine like now you have achieved that goal? How do you think about things now? Then take the Core Value Beliefs and imagine how they are now working through your day to day existence because you have achieved that goal, and concentrate on the feelings that this achievement gives you.

You will find your mind distracted and often your reasoning will speak up and tell you that your day dreaming is impossible and that it can't be achieved and you will start to look for reasons why this is a waste of time…….. Do you remember what day dreaming was? Who cares if it's real or not, just enjoy the moment. Every time the negative voice of 'reason' enters your head, just remember it's a day dream, and go back to imagining how good it could be.

It's important in this exercise that you don't put pressure on yourself that this has to be done for 20 minutes every day otherwise it's useless. I don't care if its 1 minute, literally, but what is important is that you do it every day. I have always found the best time for me was in bed at night before I went to sleep. There are no time pressures, you're generally relaxed, and it sets in motion some positive brainwaves before you go to sleep.

> *What we think, we become. Buddha*

TASK: From now on, every night before you go to sleep, pick one of your goals and just day dream about how good it would be if that was achieved. There will be some nights that are harder than others because you're tired or stressed, but give it a try even on those nights and if 1 minute is all you can do, no problem. Its consistency over the long haul that's important with everything in life….quality not quantity.

MIND
The Sixth Step on the Journey......

The Myth of Control

Everywhere we turn we are told that our future is in our hands. We are told we can become what we want, and get what we desire, if we follow the simple rules of the Law of Attraction, or practice positive awareness, or visualize daily. But why do so many people try and fail. Like everything in life, there is no black and white, and there is some truth and some bullshit in every approach to life.

> *The only things in life we have control over are, how we take action towards our goals, and how we react to circumstances beyond our control. That's it. We control nothing else. JR*

Thinking positively is an excellent approach but is not the be all and end all. Simply thinking "I am Happy...I am Happy" will not make you happy if you don't change your underlying Core Value Beliefs.

The Law of Attraction says that what we focus on we will attract, but most people interpret this as sitting and thinking about money and thinking about desires and goals and somehow they will come true. The Law of Attraction actually means that what our core (and often subconscious) beliefs and values are, is what we will attract. You may focus on a figure of $10m constantly every day, but if you have a core belief that money is only for corrupt business people....well you need to address the core belief in conjunction with the focus.

Influence

One of the problems that most people fail to understand is the complexity of the world and our level of control over circumstances. We are constantly told that our destiny is in our own hands….that is not true, but neither is the fatalist approach that our destiny is already mapped out. What we have control over is how we think, how we react to circumstances, and what actions we take. We do not have control over what other people think, how they react, or what they do.

Ultimately what we have is **influence** over our circumstances.

TASK: Look back at your goals and look at situations you know will be difficult to achieve in this process. Look hard at the situation and see clearly what you cannot control, and compare that to what you can control and what you can influence. At the end of the day it will always come down to how well you prepared with the physical and emotional tools you have available to you at that time, and how you react when confronted with various situations, conflicts, or road blocks. Things never go 100% according to plan, but it's our inability to accept that we can't control everything, which creates stress and anxiety.

When things don't go your way, when you notice you are blaming someone or something, stop and remember the Myth of Control rule, and never give up. What you must do is keep trying and influencing, but also accept that circumstances beyond your control sometimes change the result, and when that happens, adapt, adjust, and keep influencing…….but whatever you do, don't let the outcomes rule how you feel

The Domino Effect

You would have heard of the Domino effect but do you understand its metaphorical links to 'Influence' as it relates to the Myth of Control? By setting one domino in motion can create a chain reaction of dominos falling. But did you know that a single domino can knock over another domino that is approximately 1.5 times its size and mass? Let's extrapolate that. If we set one standard Domino in motion and its falls and hits a Domino that is 1.5 times its size, then that Domino falls and hits a third Domino that is in turn 1.5 times the size of the second Domino, then by the time you get to the 23rd Domino you would be able to knock over a Domino the size of the Sydney Tower or the Eiffel Tower, and by the time you get to the 31st Domino you are knocking over a Domino the size of Mt Everest!

The key here is to realise that the size of the Domino is increasing exponentially and that is exactly how your personal achievements grow as well. Start with small achievable steps and build up. Everyone overestimates what they can achieve in a year but grossly underestimates what the can achieve in 5 years.

The Butterfly Effect

The Butterfly Effect is another scientific theory that is utilised in the prediction of weather patterns and in the fascinating field of Chaos Theory. Again you have likely heard of the story whereby a Butterfly fluttering its wings in South America causes a Typhoon in Hong Kong.

The basis of the theory is that very small changes to initial conditions, can create massive changes in end results. The

Butterfly Effect could be the subject of a whole book on its own (and has been), but the importance of the theory to our lives is to understand that small changes in the way you do things can lead to massive changes in your results in the days, weeks or years down the track. This is not just a nice sentiment, it has foundations in scientific analysis and applies just as formidably to our lives as it does to a weather pattern.

The key for our lives is therefore, don't be afraid to make adjustments to our goals, or the actions we are taking towards our goals, as we learn and grow. Minor changes in strategy can have exponential impacts on the end results, and those changes need only be small....as small as Butterfly fluttering its wings.

TASK

Think about your life to date and think about some of the outcomes you have achieved, both positive and negative, and trace back through all the cause and effects and try and identify a root cause or issue that set this path in progress. Think about how that issue has been impacted by the Domino Effect and/or the Butterfly Effect. Don't lay blame on others as you work through this progress, just look at every action or decision with an impartial and unemotional view, as if you are watching a movie of someone else's life.

Now day dream about how a different decision in that moment, long ago, may have impacted where your life is now. Pick both positive and negative items so you can see the full spectrum of how these effects work.

Now that you can see how relevant and important small decisions and actions in the present are, and the impact they can have on the future, take another look at your goals and think about what actions, behaviours, or decisions you could make now, no matter how small, that could have a Domino or Butterfly Effect on your future.

MIND
The Seventh Step on the Journey......

Belief, Attitude, & Conscious Living

Beliefs

Our attitude is determined by our beliefs, and our beliefs are determined by what we have seen, heard, smelt, tasted, and felt throughout our entire life. Through our five senses we experience the world around us, and through these experiences we develop sets of beliefs about certain things. And as time progresses these experiences and beliefs become entrenched in our subconscious and are expressed in our Attitude.

> *"It's not what we know that gets us into trouble. It's what we know for sure, that just ain't so".*
>
> **Mark Twain**

In Psychology these developed attitudes are referred to as Meta-Programs. They are programmed reactions we have to certain circumstances that happen to us and situations we find ourselves in. They are subconscious programs that happen automatically and that we believe are true.

Attitude

If there's one single thing that has the biggest impact on our lives, it's our Attitude.

When we say 'attitude' we often think of a person's ego or arrogance, or 'chip on the shoulder'. As humans we always assume the negative connotation. This isn't what is meant in this context. This is all about your reaction to events beyond your control. When bad things happen, how do you react? Do you get angry, do you blame others, do you look for reasons why 'The Man' has screwed you over again?

Also at the opposite end of the scale how do you react when good things happen? I've always believed the only thing worse than a bad loser is a bad winner.

Life is not easy, but how we react to things that happen to us is the major determining factor in how we view life and to our level of happiness. Remember your perception is your reality.

I do not believe in fate, but I also do not believe we have no control. What we have control over is two key things-

1. Our attitude to a situation
2. The decisions we make in the moment

I see life as a fast flowing river and we are in a small boat with a single paddle. If we try and fight against the flow everything will be a struggle and constant failure will be your prize. However if you sit back and let the flow take you wherever it likes then more than likely the major flow leads to rapids and a crushing waterfall. But if you notice the flow of the river and don't fight it, but look ahead for the fork in the river and calm waters where you want to be, pick up your paddle, and with it start to work with the flow to change your direction. A small change in direction early leads to a big change in the final destination.

Use what tools or skills you have and work with the flow of life to influence where you end up. It doesn't mean you won't hit turbulent waters, but it's better than not having tried at all…. and who knows you might end up where you want to be.

Setting up for Failure

It's so easy to set ourselves up for failure. Expectations of who or what we should be, portrayed by the media, Hollywood, and advertising, bombard our sensibilities on a daily basis…. and none of us are immune. The plethora of goal setting and self-help books in the market place are testament to just that. They continually portray successful people and how they started from nothing and achieved greatness.

Now there is nothing wrong with striving and achieving, however our consumerist society continues to portray success as monetary wealth, materialistic gain, a perfect body, a supermodel wife, a successful musician...

So where does that leave the plumber, the electrician, the accountant, the labourer, the project manager……….it would seem from the media that these guys have underachieved. Of course it's very simple to say that is not true and materialism is not the measure of a person….but deep down we still feel less.

Setting yourself up for failure comes in different forms, including -

1. **Setting unrealistic goals** such as I want to be an astronomer, when I failed high school maths, or wanting to be the next Arnold Swarzenegger when you are 5 foot 2 inches and have a slow metabolism. You are unique and there are things you can and can't do…accept this without judgement, regret, or blame.

2. **Setting non-specific goals** such as I want to be wealthy, or I want to travel, or I want to be happy. These goals mean nothing. How much is wealthy? Where do I want to travel? What means 'happy' to

me? These goals have no destination and as such will get lost at sea. Remember our goal setting based on Core Value Beliefs from steps 2 and 3?

3. **Failing to take action**. Setting achievable goals but through a lack of motivation you do not take the required actions. This generally means your goals are not aligned with your core value beliefs.

4. **Being trapped by the outcome**. This means your happiness rests solely on achieving the outcome of the goal, and when that goal is not achieved exactly as you envisioned you are disappointed.

So how do you avoid setting yourself up for failure?

1. Firstly understand your values. You don't want a Lamborghini, you want the feeling you get from a Lamborghini. Identify that feeling.

2. Set achievable goals and take consistent action

3. Most importantly enjoy the ride. Achieving the goal is not what counts, having made the effort is all that matters.

Striving to Achieve

Western society sets a high value on striving to achieve, desire for material gains, physical appearance, and status. This is driven by our societal values which are reinforced through the media, Hollywood, and our economic system. This is in stark contrast to the eastern philosophy of acceptance of what is, where desires are seen as the cause of suffering, and quiet contemplation is considered a virtue.

Now this doesn't mean that striving to achieve is a bad thing, and it doesn't mean that a Buddhist doesn't strive to achieve, what sets them apart is how they perceive that achievement, or not, of the particular desire or goal.

In western society we consider materialism and status an integral part of who we are as a person. If we own a flash car (obviously not a Ford...) then people will consider us successful and treat us differently. What is more troubling however is that if we fail to get that nice car, then we consider ourselves a failure and a lesser person because we are not successful. The difference between this approach and the eastern philosophies is that it is recognized that desire is the cause of emotional suffering, not the fact you didn't get that car, but the suffering is caused by the importance you place on having that car and thinking that without the car you are a lesser person.

In the west our economic capitalist system is all about consumption and as such driving consumer demand is the sole focus of commercial advertising agencies. They make us relate to their products as if having that product will make us a better and more successful person. It's drilled into us from the moment we start comprehending as a child. Consumerism is not a bad thing, the way we react to it is bad.

The greatest misconception of eastern philosophies is that the elimination of desire means giving up on any goals and not striving to achieve. This is completely the wrong thinking. Elimination of desire still means you set goals to achieve, but you eliminate the attachment to the outcome. If you achieve the car or not makes no difference to who you are, what is important is that you strived and lived each moment. You do everything you can to strive to achieve, but whether you actually achieve the desired outcome is irrelevant to how you feel about yourself and who you are as a person.

Rule of Acceptance

If there's one life rule that is worth understanding and applying to your daily life, it is the "Rule of Acceptance". Acceptance of what is, Acceptance of what is outside our control, and Acceptance of people and differing views are all critical elements in how happy our day to day life is.

The critical issue with the Rule of Acceptance is in its interpretation. Unfortunately most people see Acceptance as accepting less in life, accepting that I can't control anything, accepting that I will never be rich, and therefore accepting a lower standard for myself than I would otherwise expect.

This is completely wrong. Acceptance has nothing to do with lowering your expectations. What is the problem we all face with goal setting, New Year's resolutions, and setting certain expectations for our lives? The real problem is that if we don't hit that goal right on target we get disappointed and we lose confidence and motivation. Then we stop setting goals so that we insulate ourselves from disappointment and think we are "accepting" our lot in life.

NO...NO...NO....You must set goals, you must set standards for your life, you must live your life to the fullest.

What the Rule of Acceptance means is that we carefully set goals, we set a plan of action, and we do what we can with what we have to try and achieve that goal. Beyond that there are so many external factors that we have no control over, the economy, other people's decisions, etc. that ultimately we have

INFLUENCE over the outcomes of our goals and targets but not complete control. If we had complete control everyone would have millions of dollars and be living a life of luxury.

What the "Rule of Acceptance" refers to is the outcomes of our decisions and actions. If you have tried your best, done everything you believe you could do, made adjustments to your plan when it needed, then you have done everything within your power and abilities……..so whatever happens you can accept it with the knowledge you left no stone unturned.

Acceptance becomes difficult when you know in your heart you could have done more……..but never allow yourself to be held to ransom by the things you cannot control.

Control the Controllables

Striving to achieve, the Myth of Control, The Rule of Acceptance, Control the Controllables……they are different ways of saying a very similar thing, but even though we hear them again and again in different forms, do we actually listen, or do our 'Beliefs' cause us to have the 'Attitude' that, this doesn't work for me or, people don't understand my situation? Do we decide to take action but procrastinate or try for a short time and then give it away because it's easier to stay in our comfort zone?

Control the Controllables is simply what it says…..Control what you have the ability to control, and Accept the rest as it comes. The problem for most people comes because they never truly analyse and understand what they can control. They still believe they can control what other people think, say or do, they think they can control situations around them.

Let's be very clear, when you boil it down, there are only two things you can control –

1. **The way you think in the present moment**
2. **The way you act and react in the present moment**

That's it. Simple isn't it? Well of course it isn't. Everyone knows how hard it is to change your Meta-Programs, how you think and react to a situation that is immediately in front of you. Your beliefs, that have been established over your lifetime, create your Attitude and dictate how you behave in the present moment. You react to situations based on what you perceive you have experienced in the past. This is a natural Fight or Flight type of response designed to protect you from harm. The problem is it gets so entrenched in our sub-conscious that we make assumptions about situations based on minimal facts and react in accordance with those assumptions.........but there is always two sides to every story.

Awareness & Conscious Living

But how do we change a lifetime of engrained beliefs and attitude? By waking up!

Meta-Programs are engrained beliefs and reactions to certain events that we have built up over a lifetime of experience. Meta-Programs effectively keep us asleep at the wheel of life. Now Meta-Programs are not bad, please don't misunderstand me. Without Meta-Programs we would not be able to function as the amount of information coming at us every minute of every day is too big to handle and as such 90% is dealt with by our Meta-Programs, and most of that is good. Of course the old 80/20 rule applies here, in that 20% of the information or situations coming at us, cause 80% of our problems, and it is the Meta-Programs of the 20% that we need to deal with.

There is significant discussion, books and seminars around Living Consciously these days. Again it's one of these things that (especially Old Boys), many people tend to treat as a New Age waste of time. That is a Core Belief and an Attitude in itself, exactly the thing you need to become aware of.

Overall it is quite simple, it is about recognising how you react in certain circumstances, what you believe to be true, and the Attitude that those things project. I'll give you a classic example of a major issue I struggled with for many years – Anger.

As a child I grew up in a small western Queensland town where I was not only one of the only white kids, but I was the only Ginger. It started with some teasing and general bullying, (any Ginger will understand this!!), but escalated rather quickly to physical pushing, shoving, punching. At first I didn't fight back and walked away but my self-worth took such a hammering that eventually I decided to stand and fight. Sounds like a good sensible plan. However what happened was, that despite being beaten up all the time, I found fighting back was the only way my self-worth could even remotely feel as if it wasn't completely destroyed. So I started reacting quicker and quicker. It went from reacting when someone punched me, to reacting if someone just looked at me sideways. I was constantly in fights, losing most, but in my mind defending my sense of myself. I established a belief that everyone was out to hurt me and that the only way to defend against this was to attack first.

Unfortunately this carried through into my adult life and into my business career where I just could not handle confrontation. If someone disagreed with me or challenged any decision I had made, my belief was they were out to get me and my reaction was to attack verbally and not let them get their point across. I got my way a lot of the time, but I lost a lot of respect, and of course I wasn't right all the time.

Changing my behaviour has not been easy, and there are always hints of it in the background no matter how much you mature and grow as a person. The first step is to become aware of the specific problem. For years I just blamed it on a bad temper and that was a genetic Ginger trait. But eventually you have to become aware that, for whatever reason, you have an attitude that is caused by a set of beliefs that causes you more problems than it solves. With that awareness you need to study and understand the reasons from your past, and what Meta-Program has been set up and is operating when you are faced with these situations. Becoming aware is not as simple as it sounds as when you first start you will look to place blame. Blame on your parents, your schooling, in my case on the bully's. If becoming aware of the problem is the first step, then laying blame is the second step. You are starting to understand the reasons, but need to move past the blame game. Regardless of the reasons, no matter how bad they are, you can't change them (The Rule of Acceptance), you can only change you (Control the Controllables).

Once you become aware and start to accept the reasons, the third step is to develop an action plan for when you are faced with that situation again. With my Anger, the first step I could take was only to walk away or say nothing. That was very, very hard. At first it felt like I was going backwards and letting people get the better of me, but it was the best I could do at that time as I wasn't yet strong enough to deal with confrontation in a sensible manner, the Meta-Program was too strong. But I kept at it, slipping up often, only becoming aware I was in my Meta-Program after I had verbally attacked someone, and generally finding it hard to achieve. But over time I started to see a slow change in that when faced with a situation I was able to make some reasonable responses, and eventually those responses became more frequent to the point where I can now respond to confrontation in a reasonably calm manner, and if it escalates I can generally walk away with my self-esteem in place.

But it takes Living Consciously to keep this up. You must always be aware of your present moment and how you think and react.

TASK:

Take your time over this step on the journey. There is a lot of information to digest here. Come back as many times as you need to this chapter and spend time thinking about specific situations that are impacting your life and how you can apply these set of rules to help you live a happier more peaceful existence.

MIND
The Eighth Step on the Journey......

Fear.....Do you Really Understand it?

If I ask you what you're are afraid of, you'll immediately tell me about specific things……airplanes, heights, cockroaches, New Zealanders etc. These fears are all legitimate and are real for those who suffer them but they are tangible objective fears. What do you understand of intangible subjective fears that are limiting your life? These are the fears we need to be conscious of. They are stopping you living your life to the fullest, yet we wouldn't even recognise most of them. We live our lives so unconsciously, and get caught in the constant barrage of information overload from an increasingly interconnected world, that we lose sight of the deep seated fears that are stopping us.

Key amongst these fears is the **Fear of Losing My Identity.**

As we live our lives, experience things, interact with people, face triumph and disappointment, and become more interconnected with the world, we develop a set of beliefs about ourselves that tell a story of who or what we believe we are and our place in the world. This all comes together to form our identity or 'who we believe we are'.

This identity doesn't recognise positives or negatives, it lives in our unconscious and is simply a set of beliefs that limit our comprehension of what we can and can't do. It is 'Who We Are' or our identity. For example some beliefs that others have analysed about themselves are as follows –

- I am an aggressive person
- I am a shy person
- I am good at listening to people
- I am working class
- I am a motivator
- I am a survivor
- I am a victim

Remember it's not just one or two beliefs that make up your identity, it's a multitude of lifetime experiences and influences that have created your understanding of who you are, the box within which you have placed yourself within society. Many of the beliefs about your identity cannot be exposed with some simple brainstorming, but would take months of interactive life coaching to flush out the true core of the issues.

The interesting fact is that regardless of whether the thoughts about ourselves are positive or negative, our instinct is to defend them against all attacks. But why on earth would I want to protect my identity when it is so negative? Well that comes back to our basic Fight or Flight instinct. This set of beliefs about who we are and our place in the world, positive or negative, is our identity, it is who we are, and without that identity then who are we? Do we even exist? Do we even matter? Why then are we here?

When you really start to look into yourself and understand some of your limiting beliefs, it is hard to believe how hard you work to defend them against attack from others. Just think for a moment, we have all had a time in our lives when someone has said something negative about us like "You're so negative all the time"….. "You're a real idiot"……"You never listen to anyone else's point of view"……"Your always right aren't you"…….and many more like this. What is our initial reaction? We defend ourselves against this unwarranted attack! This person doesn't know what they are talking about. They are just attacking me because they are the negative ones or the angry ones, not me!

STOP! Now just go back and look at this. 9 times out of 10 you were negative, you were an idiot, you don't listen, and you think you are always right. Yet you immediately defended against it, and you did this because your identity was being attacked, not because you were negative, an idiot, not listening etc. It was because the essence of who you believe you are was being attacked and without that, 'Who are you?'

TASKS:

Grab your note book and take some time to sit and think about situations where you feel under attack, or where you have felt criticised. What were you being criticised for? In that moment did you actually display some of those negative attributes, and you felt you had to defend yourself?

This can be a difficult task as the criticisms are emotive and you may well say the other person was wrong and you were right, but try your best to separate yourself from the situation, take a third person view, and allow yourself to be critical of your perceived identity.

Try and identify the issue that you are defending in yourself. Do you even like that attribute? Note how you subconsciously see that as part of your identification of who you are, and as such your instinctual need to defend yourself and your identity.

Fight or Flight Instinct……

The Fight or Flight reflex is generally well understood as a mental construct of survival, remaining from our 'Cave Man' days, that when faced with a dangerous wild animal, or dangerous situation, the body's reaction is to fill the blood stream with adrenalin and oxygen, in order to peak the body's performance to either Fight or Flee. It is a basic instinct survival mechanism that is hardwired into our brains. The Monty Python call to "Run away!!" comes immediately to mind.

The instinct is less relevant today as generally our basic needs of food and shelter have been met, and survival in our society is not as dangerous as our Cave Man ancestors. Having said that it is still a vital bodily function when faced with a situation that is physically endangering.

The problem is that in today's society we face few physically endangering situations, but the Fight or Flight reflex has taken on a more sinister role in western society, leading to anxiety, stress and depression.

Think about having to go into a performance review with your boss and you are worried it's not going to be as good as you want. There may be criticism of your performance and confrontation on an emotional level. You get nervous and adrenalin fills the body leading to those butterflies in the stomach and you worry about what will happen. This is the original Fight or Flight reflex in action.

The problem with today's society is that as opposed to the Cave Man days where you literally fought or ran away and utilized all that adrenalin, in today's society we don't expend that energy, either physically or emotionally, we sit quietly and smile, all the while going berserk on the inside with stress because there is no outlet.

Think for a minute about everyday things that happen, you see someone you don't like and get angry or anxious and walk across the street to avoid them. Someone cuts you off in traffic. A customer is rude and obnoxious. They all lead to a subconscious Fight or Flight reflex, which when unable to be released, leads to pent up anger and stress.

It's not something that is easy to control although meditation and other methods help, but it's a great start just to be aware the next time this happens to you, that the stress caused is a natural reaction of your body, and not a weakness on your part.

TASKS:

Take a moment to think about situations in your life that leave you anxious or stressed. Look at the real reason you feel stressed. Do you feel under attack? Do you feel you have no control over the situation? You don't really understand what is happening or being discussed, but feel like you should be able to understand or have the knowledge? You feel scared to talk in front of others and expose your perceived lack of knowledge?

There are endless situations. Make a list and think carefully about the root causes, and see how the Fight or Flight Instinct is in play. Then next time you are faced with this situation, understand that it is a natural instinct at play, and not a problem with you or your self-worth.

Fear of What Others Will Think

We tell ourselves we are independent and we don't care what others think….but that is simply not true. Like many things in life what we say and what we actually practice are two different things, and whilst we firmly believe what we say is what we do, our unconscious actions, developed over a lifetime of experiences, come to the fore when we are under stress.

That is to say, we really do give a damn what other people think and say. This is all part and parcel of the Fight or Flight reflex, of defending our identity, of who we believe we are.

When we set goals, what always stops us from taking action is the deep seated fear of 'What will others think or say about me'. It's such a core based fear that most of us aren't even aware of it, and most of us will strenuously deny that we suffer from this limiting belief. But we all do.

What if we fail?

People will talk behind my back and make fun of me.

My friends will think I've gone mad and won't want to hang out with me.

I can't do this at my age, I'll look stupid.

On the surface these seem like childish statements that we would not possibly utter….but I guarantee they are at the core of why you have unfilled aspects of your life. When something sits outside what you believe everyone agrees is 'Normal', then your fear of trying and failing, or trying and being ridiculed, will be your Great Wall of China.

When faced with this situation people always think in terms of what if I fail? Now many self-help books say you must think in terms of 'What if I succeed?', but that doesn't answer the root problem. It doesn't help me overcome my fear of failure. Yes it is good to think in positive terms and this can only help, but you know want I have found has worked for me, and helped me get outside my comfort zone……….The Adventure!

Look at what you want to achieve as a journey, an adventure to be undertaken. Then you are not bound by the success or failure of the final outcome. When you are an Old Man you can look back and say "Well that was a ride and a half" even if it wasn't successful. It gives you a story to tell, of trying, and living your life to the fullest, and not being trapped in a mundane life, lived within the parameters set by what others say is 'normal'.

I'll say it again……

"Finishing last always beats didn't finish, which always trumps never started"

TASKS:

Think about things in your life you really want to do but have not done, or things you have started but never finished. These are not material things like cars or holidays that are unachievable because you don't have enough money. These are things that are achievable and things that you like doing and want to achieve, but for some reason you just don't follow through. Some examples from others include –

- Start a Martial Art
- Learn to Play the Guitar

- Write a Book
- Study a Language
- Sing in a Band

Have a good hard look at some of your unfulfilled desires. Be honest and look at it from the perspective 'What will others think'. Is this what is stopping you?

Fear of Failure

Closely aligned with a Fear of What Others Will Think, is the Fear of Failure. What separates the Fear of Failure from other forms of fear though is it can be a very personalised and deep seated issue. It can stem from small things such as being ridiculed for a failure as a child, or a feeling of being second to a more 'successful' sibling, but it is a much more complex issue. Often one of the greatest issues causing a Fear of Failure is monetary. If I take a risk and it fails, I will lose my money and will put my family and myself in a terrible position. This is a very legitimate fear and one that often seems to be treated quite flippantly by some personal development coaches. One thing I really hate is the story of the successful person who risked it all to live his dream and now they own an Island in the Bahamas……..I mean that really gets me cranky! It's so easy to say from a position of strength that the weak person just needs to do it and stop holding themselves back.

So here's my two bobs worth on the Fear of Failure. As Old Boys, monetary concerns and risking the welfare of you and your family is the number one consideration that you need to be very clear on. Risking your life savings on living your dream and trying to make it big by turning your hobby into your fortune, is simply selfish, and if not calculated then it is tantamount to gambling. It is a very tough world out there in business and remember my discussion about the 'Myth of Control' and all the things you can and can't control?

Now to be clear, I am **not** saying you don't try, what I am saying is as an Old Boy, you are at a different stage of life than a young up and comer with no family, no ties, and nothing to lose. If you fail there are serious downsides.

What I **am** saying is two-fold –

1. Take calculated risks

This is simple and obvious. If you are looking at a new venture, take careful calculated actions. Surround yourself with people who know what you don't, and who can offer guidance and encouragement. But be careful of the people around you who are negative and simply point out what will happen if you fail. It's fine to look at the downsides and understand how you can minimise any problems, but be careful not to get caught up in negativity, and unfortunately most of that negativity will come from close family and people who maybe have a vested interest in the outcome.

The second worst type of person to have around you is the one who simply tells you what you want to hear. These people can inflate your sense of success and distort your view of the opportunity such that you may take uneducated risks.

All sounds simple doesn't it? Well it is really. Just use some common sense. My key words of advice for anyone wanting to take a risk on a new project, or new lifestyle, or business venture, would be –

- o Understand the downside. What level of downside can you live with? Minimise the downside through research and taking action

- o   Surround yourself with people who can add value to your project through both expert advice, and common sense positive encouragement

2. Fear of Failure permeates all areas of your life

Having said all that, this is the big picture issue and the one that we really need to deal with. Taking a risk on a new business venture or project as discussed above is a tangible risk with tangible downsides that we need to educate ourselves on.

The major problem though with Old Boys is how the Fear of Failure permeates all areas of our life, and we often don't even see it.

Regardless of how we came to have this fear of failure in our lives, (and its worth spending time understanding what issues from our past may have caused this automatic emotion) understand that it doesn't simply apply to big picture tangible things, it permeates our whole life. It can be evident right down to the simple things like being invited to a party where you don't know too many people, so you find an excuse not to go. A new role opens up at work which would be a promotion for you, but you find a reason not to apply. An opportunity pops up to learn a new skill, but you just can't find the time. I hear this a lot in my Old Boys Thai Boxing arena –

- "I'm too old for that shit"
- "I've got this old knee problem"
- "It's too hard with work and everything"
- "I'd love to but…."

- "I used to be able to…."
- "Back in the day…"

All these excuses are simply a Fear of Failure and a Fear of What Others Will Think. If you disagree with me then you are blind to the automatic thoughts you have. I have seen so many Old Boys eventually come along and give it a go, and I can tell you not one of them has regretted trying. They learn new skills, get fit again, and feel a sense of pride in themselves.

Now I used Old Boys Thai Boxing as a one off example but it applies to every area of your life. It doesn't have to be a major life changing event, it is fair and reasonable that major life changing events create a Fear of Failure….There's nothing wrong with that and in fact that is what will save us from making quick uneducated decisions.

What I am talking about is the simple everyday things that prevent you living and enjoying your life to its fullest.

TASK:

Think about your life and events, no matter how small or trivial, where you have said no to something that you felt you should have done, attended, or tried. Identify as many of these incidents as you can.

Now go through each one individually and look closely at the situation and ask yourself the following questions. Be truthful with yourself, be very careful you aren't justifying your decision to yourself.

- Why did I really say no? What was I scared of happening?

- Why didn't I really try? What was I scared of?
- Am I procrastinating?
- Did I just look for an excuse?

Now that you have identified some 'real' reasons, let's try and identify where those automatic emotions and thoughts have come from. Take some time to look back into your past, right back to your childhood and find times that created an intense emotion for you that aligns with these 'real' reasons. This isn't meant to be a complex therapy session that will resolve all your problems, it's simply meant to show you how some of your current thinking has become automatic and engrained in you, and what impact some past experiences have had on this.

It's all about becoming aware of things that you do and say, and behaviours that you portray, that are automatic. Becoming conscious of your actions is always the first step in change.

Other Fears….

The 4 key elements we have discussed above, are in my opinion, the foundation of the Emotional Fear Spectrum.

1. Fear of Losing my Identity
2. The Fight or Flight Instinct
3. Fear of What Others Will Think
4. Fear of Failure

There are other fears that are well documented, but all are offshoots and variations of the foundation fears. Some of the others include –

Fear of Confrontation

This has always been a major issue for me personally. As I discussed back in Step 7, as a young kid I grew up in a small western Queensland town and was the subject of relentless bullying and physical confrontation. My way of dealing with this was to fight back, which sounds good in theory but it just lead to me being bullied further because they knew they could get a reaction out of me, leading to more physical fights, and more anxiety.

In my early adult life I found it very difficult, I say nearly impossible, to accept any form of criticism as I found it was an attack on me (an attack on my identity) and my automatic emotion was fear and anger, and my automatic response was to attack. I would verbally abuse people on a level of response that was not proportional to what they had said to me, but my instinct was I had to fight back to protect myself.

As I started to deal with this I developed a fear of confrontation. Not because I was scared of the other person, but I was genuinely scared of how I would react. Even though I had started to become aware of my automatic thoughts and reactions, I still couldn't control myself in the moment.

Eventually I found a mechanism to partially deal with this, and that was to not engage, but to walk away. This wasn't ideal in a corporate environment and would leave people wondering if I was ignorant or just weak. That made me anxious and angry, but it was the only way I could deal with it.

Eventually over time I have been able to start to engage with people in a more mature way, but I am aware that this is a weakness for me and is something that I will work on for the rest of my life. But the very first step was to become aware of how I automatically reacted, and how it impacted others. Only then could I start to look at alternate ways of behaving and reacting.

Fear of Success

Fear of Success is an extension of a Fear of Failure, but it can often have its roots in an image you have built up of what successful people are, or how they have achieved their success. How often do you hear the 'Tall Poppy' syndrome in play in our society? I'm certainly not saying that all successful people are ethical and wonderful, far from it, but neither are all the unsuccessful people ethical and wonderful. There are good and bad people in every socio economic range, every race, and every religion.

But the Tall Poppy syndrome is unique in that people will look for reasons to bring down a successful person because it makes them feel better about where they are in their own lives, and provides some sense of reasoning behind why they themselves are not successful.

Be very careful with this attitude and look closely at yourself whenever you find yourself thinking like this. The only person this impacts is you. It doesn't affect the successful person. All it does is reinforce a negative stereo-type, and impact your ability to maintain a positive mentality.

Fear of Money

This is an interesting one that is sprouted often by many personal development professionals. It's closely aligned to a Fear of Success but people

> *Fear is the death of a Life Worth Living.*
>
> *JR*

aren't literally afraid of money, they are afraid of what they may lose. The more they have, the more they have to lose, and that makes them scared of losing their identity, and as such they subconsciously sabotage their progress and any potential success, and would rather live poor and unsuccessful than risking the shame of losing down the track.

MIND
The Ninth Step on the Journey......

Motivation

Why

Motivation is the 'Why' that we do something. It's this 'Why' that keeps you going when the going is tough. What most people fail to identify though is their true 'Why'.

Type 'Motivation' into Google, Facebook, YouTube, and you will be flooded with motivational websites, information, videos, quotes and so much more. How many T-shirt slogans do you see with motivational sayings? Whilst there is nothing wrong with all the motivational information available, the problem is that we treat motivation as a surface issue, something a motivational video by Ali will cure. We rely on others and external circumstances to create our motivation. The real issue is that motivation is a very personal thing. It is something that is as unique to each individual as your finger print. What motivates me, will not motivate you.

It is very easy to be motivated when things are going well, but when the path gets a little bumpy, the more solid and true that your 'Why' is, will be the difference between success and failure, between you and the person who gives up.

So how do you identify your 'Why'? This has a lot to do with your assessment of your Core Values that we assessed back in Step 2 of this journey. These are the key motivators in your life. It's so easy to get caught up in slogans and marketing, so easy to let the world tell us that we should be motivated, and then make us feel bad because we aren't, and then they sell us something that will make all your problems disappear and you will achieve your goals like never before…………..Unfortunately this is how marketing works. You need to be aware of this issue, and how you unconsciously react to the information that is force fed to you every day.

You also need to be acutely aware how much you rely on external circumstances to keep you motivated. We all have bad days, and bad periods of our lives. Old Boys are a particularly vulnerable group in my opinion, with careers, families, financial pressures, it can become overwhelming. This is why your 'Why' is so critical.

Your 'Why' in this sense, relates specifically to your goals and things that you want to achieve. Things that mean something to you. The following section will deal with areas of your life that you have to do but don't enjoy……i.e. work for a lot of us.

TASK:

Take some time to sit and think about the areas of your life where you lack motivation. Firstly assess are those areas related to your goals? Are they things that are important to you, or are they things that you feel that you have to do? Now go back and review your Core Value Beliefs. These are the root reasons you want to do something. Do you need to readjust your goal to better reflect your core value beliefs? Or do you need to change your core value beliefs because you have changed as a person, or something has moved in your life since you last assessed them?

Continue to change and reassess your goals and your core beliefs, such that they align, and you will find your motivation becomes much clearer.

Motivation when the task sucks….

But of course, in life there are a multitude of things we have to do but don't like. Work is a classic example. Of course if you don't like what you're doing, then you just resign and go out and do what you love and everything will be sparkles and ponies………………………….. If there is one thing that annoys me, it's the amount of advice given in the self-development industry about how all you have to do is follow your dreams. Now as someone who has spent a long time studying personal development, I understand that most of this advice is meant to be taken in terms of following your Core Beliefs and starting to change your attitude to the way you see life. Unfortunately though it often isn't purveyed very well to the reader. The advice is often taken literally and objectively, rather than as a guide to changing your attitude, and as such many people just switch off and say, 'well I can't do it'.

Life sucks sometimes…..and that is a scientific fact!

So what the hell do we do about motivation when we are faced with a chore that simply sucks, or a job we don't enjoy? It is a simple fact that we have to work and that is the work available now, and we can't simply up and change to a wonderful new job.

There are some extremely good lessons in Zen Buddhism that address this specific issue. I like Buddhism and Zen principles as they relate to the real world, the here and now, not the past, not the future, and are excellent methods of thinking and dealing with issues such as we are discussing.

A way people often deal with a boring or painful job is to daydream, not think about what they are doing, try and take their mind off it with social media or other. Zen Buddhism suggests we should do the exact opposite. Actually pay close attention to what we are doing. Get right into the detail. Watch the way we do the thing we are doing, do each step on the process in detail, seeing how we flow and how we think. Initially it seems that by focusing so clearly on what we are doing will only exacerbate the disdain we have for the task, but in practice is actually something quite different. And the reason is that the main issue in our disdain is that by day dreaming or thinking about other things, we are either living in the past or living in the future, and when we think about the past we start to think about things that have happened and we have regrets or wish we had done things differently, and when we think about the future we worry about what may or may not happen to us. Regret and worry…..the two great silent killers.

But by focusing absolutely on what you are doing in the moment brings your thinking to the present, where there is only what you are doing now, where there is no regret or worry.

But of course there is I hear you say. If I think about my stupid job I will get angry and stressed again. But realise that if you are getting angry or stressed again, you are linking your work to a worry about what you have to achieve, or a regret about why you are doing this, and immediately you are in the past or future again. This is why I love my Martial Arts, nothing focuses the mind to the present and makes me forget about past and future like a straight right to the face.

I'm not saying this is an easy concept to grasp let alone put into practice, but living in the present, or 'Mindfulness' as it is often called today, is one of the great skills you can learn, especially as you get older.

'You don't have to like what you do, you just need to like the way you do it'.

Motivation V Stimulation

Of course the ultimate in our life is to be able to do something for a living that we enjoy or would do as a hobby. Of course that is an unrealistic expectation for many, but be careful you are not using this as a limiting belief as well.

What we do should stimulate us in some form. It should align with our Core Value Beliefs. This doesn't mean we have to become Mother Theresa and help the less fortunate, but what does that mean in terms of the Old Boy who is a Boiler Maker for example? It means that the work you do, you do to the highest standard you are capable of. It means you keep improving your standard. It means you treat your co-workers with respect. It means you treat clients with honesty. These are simple and too often overlooked attributes in a corporate world where financial greed is the master. Financial success can go hand in hand with these attributes, but society tells us differently so we just agree and get on with our boring lives.

Don't you see how your attitude, and the way you as a person live your life, and the way you perform your day to day mundane or painful work, makes all the difference to how you view the world, and how it impacts so dramatically on your emotions of stress, anger and anxiety?

> *If you won't try hard for yourself and your own standards....then you certainly won't try hard for your team mates.*
>
> **Wayne Bennett**

Motivation comes from within. When we allow the outside world to dictate our emotions, then our motivation is simply washed away in a river of discontent.

TASK:

What do you do for a living?

What parts of what you do, do you really dislike?

Does your work align with your Core Value Beliefs?

How could you make your work align with your Core Beliefs, by changing your attitude to the way you do those things you don't like?

The Motivation Bell Curve

Motivation seems to be a true bell curve against age. Our motivation drives us forward in our youth and early adulthood, but seems to peak and begin to slide as we age. But why?

You can never point to just one element and every individual has different issues in their lives that impact their motivation –

- Physical ability
- Injury
- Health issues, weight
- Mental issues – embarrassment, fear of failure, self confidence

But much of the time it's all about our comfort zone, and everything else becomes convenient excuses for why we don't push ourselves to achieve more. Of course there are genuine restrictions of injury and health issues, BUT you must adapt both your physical world and your expectations, and realign your goals to meet those parameters, and then push forward.

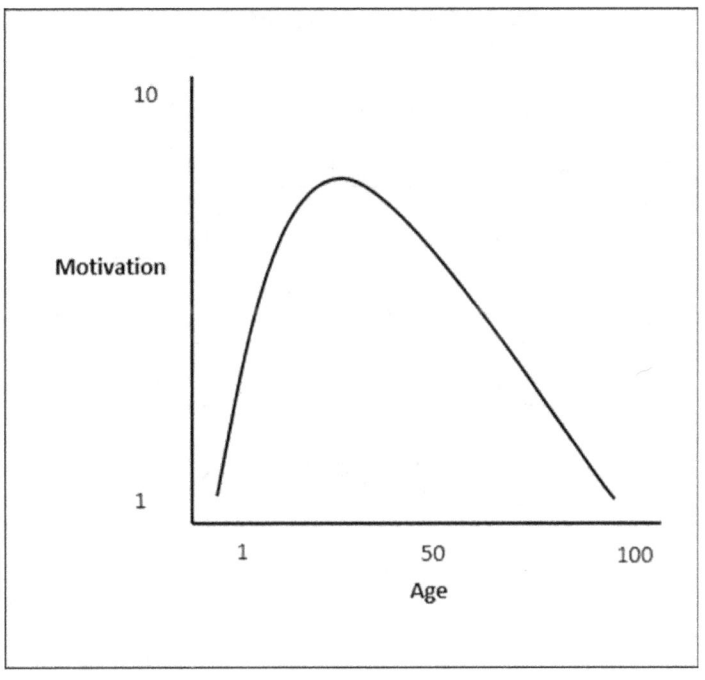

Some years ago I was working through some motivational issues and the following chart came out of that discussion. Whilst it is reflective primarily of the physical realm, many of these 'excuses' can be applied to every aspect of our life, training, health, nutrition, family and relationships. What is clear from this chart is that with men there is always a level of outward image that subconsciously needs to be maintained. It's important to not look like a sook in front of mates, and as such what I say out loud and what I actually think are two different things.

Our aim as Old Boys should be to tap into the 'What I think' elements and bring a level of acceptance to our place in the world, as with acceptance will come the dissolution of the outward excuses of 'What I Say'.

Stop talking...Stop thinking....Just Start Doing

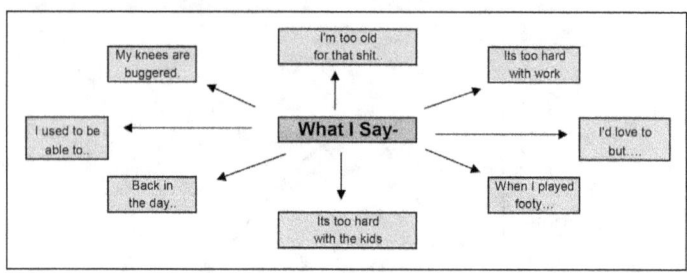

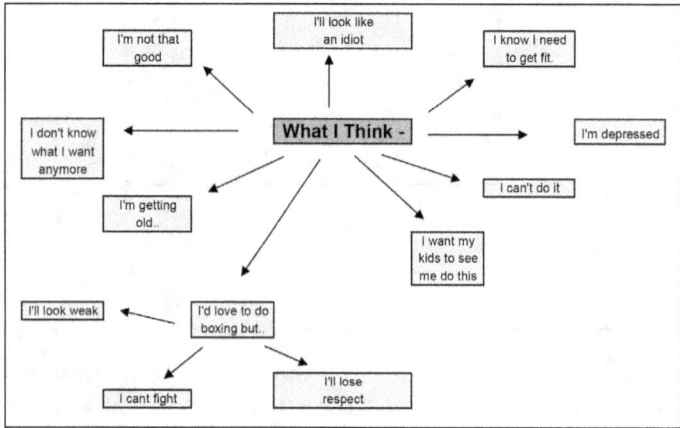

Small Steps

Another key approach to maintaining motivation is to take small steps. When the task in front of you seems too hard or too painful, or just so undesirable you can't make yourself do it, break the task down into smaller and smaller steps.

Writing this book provides an excellent example. If I was to concentrate on completing a 78,000 word book, get it proofed, published, and marketed, the task would be just overwhelming and there is no way I would ever have even started. But I put a structure in place. I set down a format, direction and topics, and then I aimed to complete a minimum of 250 words per day. Now some days even that was impossible, but the key is long term consistent action, not inflexible 'must do' goals. If I couldn't get to my writing on one day then I didn't beat myself up about it because I know that over time I was consistently trying and in the end I was achieving more than 250 words a day when I averaged it out.

Exercise is another classic example. How often do we have a workout scheduled but decide sitting on the couch with a beer or Red Wine is a far better option. Again break down the tasks to smaller outcomes. For example if your gym workout that day was 5 sets of chest and 5 sets of back, to failure, and you just can't face it. Go to the gym and just aim to do 3 sets and stop well before failure. Just take it easy.

With this approach two things will likely happen –

1. When you start you will end up doing more than you planned anyway
2. Regardless of what you end up doing you will leave with a sense of having done something, and that is better than not having done anything at all. It leaves you in a better mind space

Remember you don't have to break records every day.

Mind
The Tenth Step on the Journey......

Enjoy the Ride

Life is an adventure, a journey....it is not a destination. After all we all know how the story ends and newsflash, none of us are getting out of this alive!!

It is so easy in our everyday lives to get caught up in where we are going, the destination or the goal, and we forget to look about at where we are now. We miss so much in our lives because we are focused on something in the future, or thinking about something that happened in the past.

Enjoying the ride is called many different things -

- Live in the moment
- Be Present
- Mindful living
- Stop and smell the roses

It's one of the most common themes in personal development, that of living in the now, to stop being anxious about the future, and to stop regretting the past. But for such a simple concept, it is the most difficult to actually live.

Society puts an enormous amount of value on worrying about the future, and there is an especially greater level of

> *Do what you can, with what you have, where you are, then hang on and enjoy the ride.*
>
> **JR**

pressure and stress on an Old Boy, due to our perceived role in society as bread winners and providers. How much do we earn, can we provide for our wife/partner and children, and in hard economic times, will I have a job next week?

Many of you will read this and agree with the stresses of the modern world, but will disagree that there is anything you can do to change it. **That is exactly right!!**

There is an old saying –

If you are worried about something and you can change it, then change. If you can't change it then stop worrying.

For me I want to add to that saying –

If you are worried about something and you can change it, then change. If you can't change it, influence what you can, then stop worrying.

Remember our discussion about Influence? Controlling the controllables? You act on what you can act on, with what you have available to you, at that time. You influence whatever you can……..then you've done all you can do, so what will be will be.

What stresses us deep down is when we know we could do something differently, or we know we could have influenced something, or we could behave differently, but we don't because we procrastinate or are fearful of something. This is the real reason we can't enjoy the ride, because we are not doing everything we know we could do. When you start taking every action you can that is within your control, then the outcomes become acceptable because they are then truly out of your control.

You have to treat life as an adventure. It's up, it's down, it's challenging, it's downright hard, and it's a constant stream of good and bad moments. Think of your life as a tale of adventure. When you're 100 you want to have stories to tell, you want to be able to have really lived and experienced.

TASK:

Think about something you are worried about and write down the worry detailing what it is and why you are worried. Then ask yourself the following questions –

- Is there some other action regardless of how small (in fact the smaller the better as this engenders a sense of achievement and builds momentum by taking small steps) I can take towards resolving this worry?

- Is there a behaviour I can change that will influence the way I view this worry?

- Is there an associated element, person, or thing that I can act on that whilst not directly related to the main worry, could influence the outcome?

Now be very truthful with yourself in the next two questions –

- Am I procrastinating on doing something I know will help with this worry?

- What am I afraid of that is stopping me taking an action, or changing a behaviour, or influencing associated things? (Go back to the list of Fears in Step 8)

MIND
The Eleventh Step on the Journey......

Adjust your rudder

I like to think of life as a big river, and we are a small row boat on that river. We are constantly making our way down river and stopping at various ports along the way. The river is hugely wide in some parts, small and narrow in others, fast flowing in areas, and slow and calm in others. There are rapids, waterfalls, heavy vegetation hanging out into the river, and hidden rocks under the water. The weather is hot and sunny some days, cold and windy others, and can be stormy and fearful at times.

Our job is to navigate the river downstream to the open sea. We don't know how long the river is, we just know the direction the water flows.

Remember we are only a small boat in a large and powerful river. You'll often hear people say to swim against the current, be your own person, go your own way, make your own path. I think a little differently. In a strong and powerful river, trying to row against the current will see you either stay in the same place, or make very small headway for a lot of effort. Why not turn and go with the current, but adjust your course as you go. Let the strength of the flow of the river provide you momentum to change course and make big changes in direction with much less effort. Martial Arts has a very similar philosophy, especially Arts such as Aikido and Wing Chun. Don't fight a strength game against a stronger opponent, use their strength and momentum and turn that into a win.

Our journey on the river of life sees us pull into various different ports over time, for shelter and comfort. These ports represent, elements of our lives where we feel at ease, and are times when we feel sheltered from the ravages of day to day life on the river. Staying in a port for a while is good as it rejuvenates us. But staying in a port too long could easily become our comfort zone, procrastination or perhaps a fear of what lies ahead on the river. Old Boys can easily stay in the 'Port of Mid-life' where it's comfortable, there's food, there's beer, and it's fun. But there's also no exercise, there's laziness, excuses, and depression. You know in your heart when you've been in port too long, but will you set sail again?

When you decide to leave port and continue your journey, make sure you plan though. Leaving port without a map of where you are going can be fun for a while, but it quickly turns to either boredom as you have no goal, or to terror as you hit the rapids without a plan. Firstly understand why you are leaving Port (your Core Vale Beliefs), understand where you are going (Goal Setting), understand how you will get there (An Action Plan), and be prepared to adjust the rudder to suit the conditions on the river (Influence).

When you are out on the river and the current is so strong you are struggling to deal with your direction and where you want to go, remember at times like this all you do is influence the direction. You want to head for a shallow calm spot you can see ahead, so adjust the rudder early and keep an eye on the goal. Remember small changes in a strong current can make a big difference downstream.

And then there are the rapids. We all know these times in life when control and even influence are almost non-existent. Its times like this you just hold on. Bring in the oars and fasten

Adjust your rudder

down your load, and just let the rapids take you. Don't fight against the rapids, you'll be surprised that the fast flowing water will know the best way through, it's your job to hold on and still be in the boat when you come out the other side.

Be always aware of your surroundings. When you are out in calmer waters and drifting along on a nice sunny day, it's easy to drift off towards the bank and get entangled in overhanging branches. Always keep your awareness of your Core Value Beliefs and your Goals. It's as easy to get lulled into a comfort zone in calm waters as it is to get stuck in a port. When sailing is smooth don't stop adjusting the rudder. Don't become complacent, put yourself in the best position for the rapids ahead. The open sea is the end of your life…So keep adjusting the rudder, keep looking at how you act, behave, and live, and make adjustments based on what you know and what you have available to you at that time. Remember every day you get older you have more experience and more ability to make adjustments to your life.

> *"Be water my friend".*
> **Bruce Lee**

In the end you can find a port and settle down, live a safe and non-remarkable life, and die in that port. But in the end is that the story of adventure you want to be able to tell when you reach the open sea?

MIND
The Twelfth Step on the Journey......

Remember why....

And we come back to the beginning. It's the why in life that is the most important. Living an *Old Boys* life is not about material gains, it is not about money, it's not about status. It's all about how life makes us feel, it's about how we treat ourselves and how we treat others. It's about living by the Warrior Code, living as a genuine man who can hold his head high in any company regardless of status, and living a life of adventure.

> *Make your 'Why' strong and never forget your 'Why'*
>
> *JR*

Your Core Value Beliefs are the most important element you need to understand. They are what make you tick, and what motivates you. As *Old Boys* we are at a different stage of life to younger men. Ego is far less important, and looking for meaning in a world that puts such economic and emotional pressures on men, is the key to taking back control and Living a Life Worth Living.

BODY

Drowning

I woke up one morning
From a dream I was drowning.
Washed up on the shore
Breathless and floundering.

My world was an Island
I was locked in a cage
My life had capsized
On the rocks of age.

My body was weak
Not the prime of my youth
But I'm not an old man
Was all I could think.

I hadn't noticed at all
The slow declining
Of my health and my body
From years of denying.

The years of drinking
And eating for fun
And ignoring my body
Content in the sun

Body

And now I walk slower
And I look for applause
For the older I get
The better I was.

JR

Body
The First Step on the Journey....

What is Old Boys Health & Fitness, and Why We Must Change?

Being an Old Boy can be a testing time in your life. You still think young. It only seems like yesterday that you were playing sport, running up and down ladders, and working out regularly, but life has gotten very busy and priorities change. This is a normal stage of life with growing families and careers. The problem lies in our mental state and the gap between what we think we can do and what we can do physically. Our mental ability starts to exceed our physical ability and what generally happens with Old Boys is that a few injuries start to occur, and we decide to either give it all away, sit on the couch and live on the stories of past glory, or we push through the injuries with dogged determination, get reinjured and push ahead again, until we get so frustrated……we give it all away, sit on the couch and live on the stories of past glory.

Don't be the guy who the older he gets, the better he was.

The 5 Keys to Physical Change

There are 5 key areas we need to address in our quest for physical longevity and change –

1. Ego
2. Breaking Records
3. Consistency

4. Motivation
5. Nutrition

Ego

It's a time when our ego becomes vulnerable. A time when our sense of identity, of who we are, is brought into question. We used to be able to do certain things. We used to be able to lift certain weights. We used to be able to run that far. All our physical abilities start to become vulnerable to past injuries and new injuries. We ache in places we haven't ached before. We take twice as long to recover from setbacks. Our time is more limited as our priorities and responsibilities have changed with family and work commitments. All these elements take a toll on our ego. They question our abilities and can lead to a level of depression if left unchecked and if we don't adapt to our changing body.

Breaking Records

There was a time when every time we visited the gym we aimed for a new bench press record, or we looked for a new best time on our 5km run. But now every time we visit the gym or run we seem to be going backwards. This is the stage of our lives where our mental state has drifted far ahead of our physical ability to train and recover. The key is to become conscious of this process, accept the process, and manage your body to achieve a consistent long term approach.

Consistency

Consistency is the key. You won't break records every day. Understand that if you continue to push the boundaries, and you don't adapt to your changing situation, then you are on a short term path to injury, health issues, and depression. You must develop a total body program that addresses the key fundamentals that you can continue to do with consistency over the longer term.

Motivation

As we grow older our motivation seems to disappear as well. But what is actually happening is that our priorities have changed. As a younger man the motivation to be fit and healthy and look good is certainly higher than the fear of the pain of the training to follow. As Old Boys our focus is on different aspects of our lives, work/career, family etc. We'll talk more about motivation in terms of our physical health later in this section but at this stage it is enough to understand that motivation hasn't deserted us, it has just changed its focus as our priorities in life change.

Nutrition

Nutrition has been left to last for a reason……its 80% of our problem! We all know that the biggest issue we face is our diet, but for the love of god we can't seem to say no to those chocolates, or that second/third/fourth beer.

There is of course an uncontrollable major problem with getting older and that is our metabolism slows down, we simply don't burn as fast as when we were younger and hence it takes more effort on our behalf to burn the same calories than a guy 20 years our junior.

However when you boil it all down, Old Boy nutrition consists of two key problem areas –

1. The type of foods we consume and the balance of Carbs, Proteins and Fats and;

2. Portion Size

We constantly tell ourselves we are starting to eat properly tomorrow.....but tomorrow just never comes. For such a major issue for our health and well-being it's amazing we just can't follow a decent eating pattern isn't it? Well therein lies part of the problem. We put so much emphasis on our diet, we see it as the most important thing, and subconsciously if it's not perfect then we've obviously failed, and when we fail we get disheartened. The pain of trying to eat healthy becomes greater than the desire to be healthy. The short term gratification of that chocolate and/or beer is a greater attraction than the potential pain of diabetes or cholesterol or heart disease in years to come.

Again we'll get into detail on what I have developed as *Old Boys Nutrition Planning* later in this chapter, but just keep one simple rule in mind at this stage....stop making it such a big deal and take the pressure brake off.

TASK:

Have a look at your own life.

Where have you come from? What sports did you used to play? What did you do for physical activity that you now no longer do because of time/motivation/injury or other?

Be honest with yourself, what part does your ego or your sense of who you are, play in where you are now?

Look at your motivation, what part of your life has your motivation transferred to now?

Look at your nutrition and daily diet. What do you eat? How big are your potions?

Keep on Punching.....

BODY
The Second Step on the Journey....

Let's Take a Physical Inventory

Just as we did in the MIND section, the first step is to take an honest inventory. Note I said 'honest'. It's interesting that when we look at our 'Mind' we tend to be hard on ourselves, negative, and don't give ourselves much credit for strengths. But when we look at our Body and Nutrition we constantly fool ourselves about what we are eating, how much we are eating, our fitness levels, exercise consistency, and our general view of how good we are.

Why are we so negative on one element of our lives and yet seem to cut ourselves slack in another area?

For Old Boys it's all about how we perceive a man should be in modern society. Its poor form to talk about your feelings and emotions, and makes you less of a man if you do. On the other hand it's also considered unacceptable to talk yourself or your strengths up, especially the intangible mental and emotional strengths. But when it comes to body, the ego gets in the way. We don't want to admit too much physical weakness. We are loathe to come to the realisation that we can't do the physical things we used to be able to do. Our deep seated Survival Instinct has a need to confirm that we are strong, able to defend ourselves against harm, and can survive anything thrown at us.

If we are going to take an 'honest' physical inventory, we need to be conscious of the impact the ego and the survival instinct has on our subconscious. We need to be aware when we are fooling ourselves, and when we are distorting facts to suit our vision of who we are as a person.

So with that in mind……

TASK: Where are you at?

Its Physical Inventory time. Answer the following questions honestly.

- What physical activity or training do you currently undertake?

- How many times per week do you train?

- When you train what level of intensity do you train at with 1 being sitting on the couch drinking beer, to 10 being throwing up from intensity!

- What is your current weight?

- What weight would you like to be at on a comfortable day to day basis? (Note this is not exclusively overweight, a more healthy weight for some people may be more than where they are at the moment. Skinny is not automatically healthy)

- Have a look at your current diet. Look closely at the last week and write down everything you have eaten

- Then set yourself the task of writing down everything that passes your lips for the next week (including water…don't leave anything out).

- At the end of the week go back and compare what you said you had the week before to what you actually had and see the differences. See where you are kidding yourself!

- Look at your portion sizes. Remember a Portion of food is roughly the size of your palm, but it can depend on the food type so do some research. Have a look at each food group and see where you sit. There will be more on Portion Size and Control further in this chapter.

Identify Limitations and Restrictions

As Old Boys we've all got limitations and restrictions, physical and mental. There are two things that we tend to do that limit our ability to keep to a regular physical health schedule, and they are polar opposites in their nature -

1. **IGNORE** - We ignore the injury or the restriction and we push through. We push ourselves harder and call ourselves out as weak for not trying hard enough if we start to fall behind.

2. **EXCUSE** - We use our injuries and restrictions as an excuse not to push ourselves, and we succumb to the first sign of strain and use that as an excuse not to train

It's important that you recognise both of these restrictive mind sets and see them for what they are, which is a mindset that has served you well in the past, but now may need adjustment as you grow older.

To ignore injury and push through is a symptom of the Old Boy who was once a competitive sportsman and who is at that stage of life where mental expectation is starting to exceed physical ability. As discussed earlier this is a delicate time of life and if not handled properly can lead to long term injury, depression and related health issues.

The excuse approach can be seen in two streams of Old Boy –

1. The Old Boy who was competitive but has recognised his physical limitations and is not prepared to be seen as unable to compete as they used to, so uses injury and restrictive excuses to not compete and lives on the stories of the glory days or;

2. The Old Boy who was never sporty or competitive and who may have always used some form of excuse not to compete to avoid a subconscious fear of being embarrassed

What is critical is to recognise where you fall in these categories and understand that none of these are a failing or a reflection of you as a person. These narratives or stories we tell ourselves about who we are, are constructed over a lifetime of experiences and can become so entrenched we identify with that story as a critical part of who we are. Remember our discussion about our inability to let go of 'Who we are' as without those stories we will feel we have lost our identity and therefore, who are we?

I can't emphasise enough two key elements here –

1. Be honest with yourself and recognise where you fall within this analysis and;

2. Do not see this as a weakness on your part. It is simply how you have been moulded over time, but that it is something that with a few tweaks of attitude, can lead to major changes in your life and health.

Let's Take a Physical Inventory

TASK:

Have a close look at your past, were you competitive or not?

How did you face up to your physical fitness and to physical challenges?

How is that impacting on how you behave now when it comes to your physical fitness and well-being?

Where would you like to be?

So you've assessed where you are and what your restrictions and limitations are, now it's time to look at where you want to be. The big problem most Old Boys face here is over estimating where they can be in 12 weeks and underestimating where they can be in 12 months.

12 weeks seems to be the miracle timeframe in the fitness industry. Everyone has a 12 week body challenge, and the before and after shots of successful people are incredible and enough to make an Old Boy just want to give up and crack a beer. The issue we as Old Boys face is where we are at our stage in life and our changing motivations, as we've already discussed. So my answer to this is –

Think long term…..Act short term.

By this I mean look at where you want to be in 12 months, not 12 weeks. Make your goal realistic and achievable, then set an action plan based on a week by week basis. After you've set your 12 month goal, you don't look at that again until months 3, 6 and 9, at which time you review your actions against your progress, and make adjustments where needed.

Think long-term,
Act short-term

JR

Your action plans are set for the week ahead and look no further than the day in front of you. If you go back and review the Goal Setting exercises in the 'Mind' section, the same principles apply to physical goals as for monetary or any other. Your goals must be specific, achievable, measureable, and able to be broken down into small tasks or 'mini' goals.

When thinking about where you want to be, forget thinking about getting back to where you were when you were 20. Now that sounds like a common sense thing to say but I guarantee most Old Boys will look at where they were when they were 20 then either think they can get there, go hell for leather, and then give up. Or acknowledge they can't get there, and then give up. We're such a vain simple bunch really!

Look at what you enjoy doing in terms of sport or exercise and try to incorporate that into your fitness routine. Don't think it all has to be boring cardio or weights, it has to have a level of pleasure otherwise it becomes too hard to stay motivated. As you will see further into this book, my fitness is based around Boxing and Muay Thai skills. I'm a huge fan of learning a skill that gets you fit, rather than just going through the grind of weights or aerobics. This is how my *Old Boys Thai Boxing Club* has emerged. The boys want to get back in shape but just can't motivate themselves for the traditional gym sessions. Learning to fight and learning a skill is something to grab onto as we get older, and is an incredible motivating factor to keep you going for the long term.

Set your goals for different areas such as –

- Run/Walk a certain distance in a certain time
- Number of body weight reps

- Able to complete 5 x 3 minute heavy bag sparring rounds

I recommend setting multiple physical goals as we get older as it provides a broad fitness base and it helps avoid boredom and lack of motivation by keeping things always fresh.

You will also see much written about how you must not run after a certain age, or you shouldn't lift heavy weights, or you shouldn't do high impact sports. There is no right or wrong based on age, only right or wrong based on your restrictions, limitations and desires as an individual. For example I used to be a reasonable runner in my teenage years but when I hit 40 years old my knees started to get sore when I ran, so I needed to adjust. For me it meant a 20 minute combined walk/run session instead of a consistent 5km run. You however may be running marathons and if that works for your body then keep doing it.

TASK:

Look closely at your ideal fitness level, physical look, and skills you want to achieve. Brainstorm your ideas and your ideal vision for yourself.

Now look closely at your limitations and restrictions. How does your desired outcome fit around these elements? Don't rule things out because of your limitations or injuries, look for alternatives. Look to change the way you do that certain thing so you can still enjoy it and set a goal, but perhaps you do it differently to others. In my *Old Boys Thai Boxing* classes we focus on the Muay Thai skill of Hands, Elbows, Knees and Legs as weapons, but I have several Old Boys with knee problems for example, so these guys work hand and elbow skills and utilise strong side knees with methods that are still effective for self-defence or sparring. They don't give up, they adapt and work around their limitations.

Now from this brainstorm set yourself some specific goals for 12 months. These can include anything you like, don't be restricted by what you think others may expect of you. Goals can include the traditional such as –

- Walk/Run distance or time
- Weight goal
- Body measurements

Or they can include adventure goals such as –

- Be able to trek a certain adventure trail you've always wanted to do
- Mountain bike a specific trail
- Enter a Triathlon or Adventurethon
- Or a multitude of other goals. Think what you would love to experience or do and make that your fitness goal and structure your fitness routine around it.

Equating the Gap

Remember our Goal Setting methodology? We've established where we are, we've established our limitations, and we know where we want to be. Now let's assess that information and Equate the Gap.

Equating the Gap is a critical phase in understanding the gap between where we are and where we want to be. Without critically assessing that gap, we are in effect driving a rudderless ship. Yes we know where we want to get to, but we don't have a map. No destination is ever reached in a straight line, it's a series of adjustments and allowances for conditions and circumstances, and as such by Equating the Gap we are mapping out our course.

It's at this stage we want to take a careful inventory of our strengths, and of the opportunities that are available to us. Everyone is aware of a traditional SWOT analysis (Strengths, Weaknesses, Opportunities and Threats), well we've identified our limitations and restrictions (Weaknesses and Threats), and its time now to identify our Strengths and Opportunities.

Strengths, on face value, are the physical things we can do now, the abilities we have, and how we can adapt our bodies and exercise routines to meet the demands that our goals will expect of us. But when we dig deeper it's important to understand our mental and emotional strengths. What do we enjoy doing, and adapt that to an exercise routine. When are we at our most motivated, mornings or evenings, and structure our workout times around that. Who are the people who we know will support us in achieving our goals? Who are we prepared to share our goals and desires with? Surrounding yourself with people who love and support you will be a critical element of the emotional journey you are embarking on.

Don't under estimate how big an emotional journey the physical journey is. People tend to think of it as purely doing the exercises and eating the right foods. Tangible things that can be controlled. But what controls us is our emotions. When you enter into a new phase of your life and are looking to achieve a new level of health and fitness, it all generally starts off in a blaze of glory. Motivated to the hilt, you power into the training and the diet and over the first few weeks things are looking great. But then it becomes routine and a little mundane, and the gains start to slow, and this is where our emotions start to take control. "This is too hard". "It's not worth the effort". "Why am I doing this at my age?" All the reasons start to be generated by our emotions as your mind starts to look for the comfort of where it used to be. This is the make or break and if you have shared your goals and desires with a loved one or trusted friend, this is when that will be invaluable to you. The kind of motivation that comes from a friend with genuine hope for your health and well-being, trumps the screaming and yelling of a drill sergeant PT instructor every time.

TASK:

So from the previous section, revisit and write down your goal or where you want to be, and also write down where you are at.

Then take a good look at your strengths. What are you good at? What do you enjoy? When do your work and family commitments allow you to train? What can you do to change your daily routine to make sure your workouts become a priority and a firm part of your life?

Then ask yourself who you would share your goals and desires with? It's difficult sometimes for Old Boys to share their personal goals for fear of ridicule, but you will be amazed the support you receive when you do share.

BODY
The Third Step on the Journey....

The 4 Physical Pillars

Too often we focus on one area of our physical health and neglect others. When we were younger and we focused on a particular sport or activity, we were able to get away with partial neglect of other areas because we were young and able to adapt and recover quickly. Old Boys however need to be smart and start to look at physical health with a holistic approach. Continuing to focus on one area of health at the expense of others is a clear recipe for problems down the track. Injury, cholesterol, diabetes, are all things that start to creep up on us and by the time we realise we have a problem it can often be a little too late.

There are 4 Physical Pillars an Old Boy must address and have a plan for. You might well enjoy one more than the other, and one will always be harder than another, but I can't stress enough how important it is to have an action plan for all 4.

The 4 Physical Pillars –

1. **Strength**
2. **Stamina**
3. **Flexibility**
4. **Nutrition**

Strength

Maintenance of strength as we grow older has close links to issues such as bone density and joint health, but more importantly for Old Boys is the emotional connection to our manhood and being able to continue to train and have a level of strength as we grow older.

It's important to understand that as we grow older we have to adapt our understanding of strength to match our physical body. Strength, for many men, is all about how much weight you can lift, and that attitude needs to change. Body weight exercises and machine controlled weights are as effective at growing and maintaining muscle as we grow older as heavy weights when we were younger. Old Boy strength is based around core strength, joint strength, and major muscle group strength, in a balanced approached so that one area isn't stronger or weaker than another. It's all about longevity.

Stamina

The immediate thought on stamina is I need to be able to run 5km at least. That is one type of fitness but I suggest is not the best form of fitness for the average Old Boy. Stamina has always been a horses for courses approach. Boxer's stamina is completely different to long distance runners, which is completely different to a weight lifters stamina. Stamina comes in many forms.

The Old Boy way is based on shorter periods of activity with shorter breaks, over a set period. It aligns very much with our Boxing and Muay Thai training and includes interval training, high intensity and short breaks to build stamina.

This doesn't mean that running 5km is not good if that's what your body can handle but again it's all about longevity and being able to sustain a level of stamina over the longer term of your life.

Flexibility

Flexibility is an absolute essential as we grow older but unfortunately it is the most neglected and the most misunderstood.

At best stretching sometimes means a few touch toes before training and then a few touch toes after training. Let's face it, when we were younger stretching was far from a priority. These days there is much more emphasis on it but it still remains a misunderstood and neglected activity.

Old Boy flexibility revolves around some key areas –

- Dynamic Flexibility
- Static Flexibility
- Joint and Rotation Flexibility
- Yoga

These will be explained in detail further in this chapter.

Nutrition

Aaahhh……my weakest area. But in my defence, it isn't my fault. I'm married to a Sicilian who is the best cook ever, so I blame her.

Nutrition is the most well documented and discussed element of fitness there is. There is so much literature and education available, and to be fair most Old Boys have a reasonable knowledge of Diet, Carbs, Proteins, and Fats etc. But the problem lies in information overload. There is so much information and so many ways of doing things that it gets confusing and it's so easy to give up on.

The Old Boy way is based on the KISS principal (Keep It Simple Stupid). It revolves around some key areas including –

- Understanding Carbs, Fats, Proteins, Sugars
- Number and timing of meals during the day
- Portion size
- Vice Recognition

This will all be explained in detail further on in this section, but it is sufficient for now to understand that the principal is to keep things simple……and as Old Boys we still enjoy our beer, wine and food!

BODY
The Fourth Step on the Journey....

The 'Menu' Approach to Health & Fitness

As we grow older we need to approach our physical health in a different manner, but it's not just a simple change from one type of exercise to another, it's about constantly listening to our bodies, adapting the way we do things, and overcoming obstacles in a smart way…..not in the testosterone fuelled way of our youth.

We have to be smarter about our choices, and be prepared to learn new ways of doing things. Unfortunately what happens a lot of the time is we get some injuries, try and push through because we don't want to be a wimp, get reinjured, get frustrated and eventually decide it's easier to sit down with a cold beer and talk about how good we used to be.

Over the years I have played Rugby League, competed in Athletics, and been heavily involved in various forms of Marital Arts. Sports like Rugby League are generally a younger man's game and at the very least have a limited life span in terms of the body's ability to cope with the constant high impact on joints and muscles. The Old Boys approach I have developed is based on my experiences in dealing with a changing body and changing motivations. Its core lies in higher repetitions, lower resistance, with shorter rest periods, but combining this with learning skills and enjoying what you are doing.

> *"Improvise, Adapt, Overcome".*
>
> **Sgt Gunny Highway, Heartbreak Ridge**

The core elements of the Old Boys approach to Health and Fitness is based on the 4 Physical Pillars as described in the previous chapter, and further dissected as follows –

- Warm-up
- Strength and Conditioning
- Stamina and Aerobic Fitness
- Flexibility, Warm-Down, Yoga
- Nutrition, Diet and Supplements

The methodology utilised in the Old Boys approach to Health and Fitness, is to allow each Old Boy to build their own selection of exercises and activities that they can choose from every session. The reasons for building a 'Menu' of exercises and activities is to counter the following issues –

- **Injuries and Limitations** – Each of us are different and we have different backgrounds, and different injuries and limitations. What works for me won't necessarily work for you. So build your Health and Fitness 'Menu' around exercises that work for your body type

- **Time Constraints** – We are all busy. Work and family commitments at this stage of our lives can be problematic and can be almost all consuming at times. By being able to choose from 5 minute workouts through to full blown gym sessions allows us to work within our Time Constraints and not use them as a convenient excuse

- **How you feel Physically** – There are some days when you are due for a full workout but you are still sore from a previous workout, or there is a niggling injury that is frustrating you. By being able to change your workout and exercises, by selecting from the 'Menu' allows you to work around your physical state on a day by day basis

- **How you feel Emotionally** – There are days when we are physically ok but we just can't face a full blown gym workout. We are emotionally drained from work or family or other issues. We all know a workout will do us good but we just can't face it. At times like this just pick one or two exercise from the Menu that will take you a few minutes. It will give you a sense of having done something and is always better than doing nothing because you can't face the full workout.

  At the opposite end of the scale you may start the day's workout and feel really great. Take advantage and keep going by selecting another exercise or two from the Menu and work that bit harder.

- **Motivation** – By having choice and being able to change exercises regularly really helps combat a lack of motivation that can come from doing the same thing over and over again.

The Old Boys Menu methodology works with all these limitations by –

- Reducing load, increasing repetitions, reducing rest time
- Deflecting load from joints and tendons

- Increasing resistance through reduced rest time

- Setting clear parameters for manageable increase in load that protects joints and reduces downtime due to injury

- Turns the traditional setting and tracking of goals on its head

- Takes a hard look at the 'Why' which is the only real motivator

Reducing Load

The first step is to reduce the load you are putting on your joints. What tends to happen is that when we are young and at our strongest we can lift heavy with good form that puts all the pressure onto the muscle not the joint. As we get older and our strength, almost imperceptibly, starts to wane, our form starts to drop and we start to use momentum to move the same weight we did before. This loss of form then transfers more and more load onto the joints and tendons. Often it takes an injury before we are prepared to admit we can't lift the load we used to.

Increasing Repetitions

As load is reduced repetitions will increase, but regardless of the increase in repetitions, good form must remain central. The Old Boys methodology is based on 5 sets of a single exercise with a 15 second rest (see *Increasing Resistance through Rest Time Reduction* below). Enough resistance should be applied such that a minimum of 50 repetitions can be done over the 5 sets. If you can't do 50 then you reduce the load, or change the exercise to an easier version and work up. If you can do, or if you achieve, 100 repetitions in the 5 sets then the load should be increased to reduce back to just above 50 and keep building that way.

Increasing Resistance through Rest Time Reduction

It's important to understand though that reducing load does not have to mean reducing resistance. Resistance in the old boy's methodology is increased through reducing rest time. The exercises become more intense by limiting the oxygen to the muscle group by reducing rest time. Yes you will lose strength, but that is part of the aging process that you have to accept, and I'm not saying you go from a 100kg bench press to a 20kg bench press overnight, it is a gradual process that works with your own body and how it feels. Everyone is different and you may still be lifting 90kg at 60 years of age and if that works for your body that is great, just make sure you are doing it with good form and preventing injury, and not doing it just out of a sense of 'look at me' ego.

How Often Should I Train?

The older we get the more we need to listen to our bodies when it comes to how often we should train. Having said that though the philosophy of the Old Boys methodology is to maintain the consistency but alter the intensity as required. For example you have trained for 4 days so far this week and you are due to do a 'Bag Man' session but you notice your elbow joints are a little sore. Instead of using that as an excuse to not train that day, go to the 'Menu' and choose a different workout or a different level of exercise that you can do that day that works around the sore

Maintain consistency, alter intensity.

JR

areas. It may be that you decide a Yoga workout is the best for you that day, or that a 5 minute 'Quickie" is all you can achieve. It's all about doing something no matter how small, and building a consistent approach to your training, rather than high intensity workouts then rest for 3 days because you are so sore or injured, or using travelling for work as an excuse not to do anything.

Having said that a good solid training schedule should include 2 Stamina workouts per week, 2 Strength workouts per week, and 2 Yoga sessions per week. An example of a schedule may be as follows –

DAY	WORKOUT	COMMENT
Monday	Strength – The Works	
Tuesday	Stamina – Boxing Training	
Wednesday	Yoga	
Thursday	Strength – The Quickie	Travelling away for work
Friday	Stamina – The Quickie	Travelling away for work
Saturday	Yoga	
Sunday	REST DAY	

The beauty of the Old Boys system is that you can plan for the week, but make changes every day, that suit your busy lifestyle, by choosing from the 'Menu'. I set my weeks training routine every Sunday so that I am ready to go for the week ahead, but adapt every day dependent on the circumstances I find myself in that day. To do this I use the **Menu Planner** as my guide.

Old Boys

The Menu – Exercise Planner

1. **Select your workout for the day**
   - Strength & Conditioning
   - Stamina
   - Yoga
2. **How much time do you have to workout?**
   - Allow 10 minutes for warm up and warm down
3. **Select an exercise from each body part, dependent on how much time you have.**

   Allow

   5 minutes for Warm Up

   5 Minutes per body Part

   5 minutes for warm down

NOTES

1. Exercises are done for 5 sets at a resistance that allows a minimum of 50 total reps and a maximum of 100 total reps for the whole 5 sets
2. Resistance is adjusted up or down depending on when reps are below 50 or over 100
3. Rest period is 15 seconds between sets
4. Aim for 2 Strength workouts, 2 Stamina workouts, and 2 Yoga workouts per week
- **Listen to your body BUT…Don't make excuses**

BODY
The Fifth Step on the Journey....

The Warm-Up

The warm-up is something that is always taken for granted and is boring and often brushed over with a few star jumps at best, but as we get older I can't stress enough how important the warm-up is. Our joints, especially knees and shoulders, have been worn down with years of activity and our cartilage doesn't provide the buffer between bones it used to. Old injuries can cause muscles to freeze joints in positions that are comfortable when we are at rest but can easily become torn muscles, tendons or joint damage if we don't warm-up properly.

Firstly I want you to understand the difference between **Static** stretching and **Dynamic** stretching. An excellent reference on stretching is a book called 'Stretching Scientifically' written by Thomas Kurtz. It provides an excellent and detailed analysis of all the different types of stretching and how and when they should be used or are most effective. For us Old Boys the two key stretching methods we need to be aware of are Static and Dynamic.

In simple terms Static stretching is touching our toes and holding, or any stretch that is done where a stretch is held in a motionless or Static position.

Dynamic Stretching is shoulder rotations or leg raises or any stretch that is done while maintaining the stretched area in motion.

I'm not going to go into the scientific detail of how and why these stretches are best for various situations. It is enough for us to understand this basic principal –

- Dynamic Stretches are done at the beginning of a workout as part of the warm-up and Static Stretching is done at the end of a workout as part of the warm-down.

Now dynamic stretching must not be confused with Ballistic Stretching. The difference between the two is control. Let's take front leg raises as an example. If you raise your leg in front at medium pace, all the while controlling the motion with your muscles, and lowering down under control of the muscles, this is Dynamic stretching. If you throw the leg up using momentum this is Ballistic Stretching. Ballistic Stretching can have a place but only for motions that are well trained by the person. As we get older Ballistic stretching is the quickest way to torn muscles. Ensure you MAINTAIN CONTROL through Dynamic Stretching and don't slip into Ballistic stretching because you are lazy.

Dynamic stretches cover every area of the body and should cover all your joints from the ankles up to the neck and then a few dynamic stretches that mimic the activity you are about to do. For example before I do a Muay Thai or Kick Boxing workout my warm-up and Dynamic stretching routine looks something like the following –

- Walk for 1 minute while shaking loose hands, wrists, elbows, shoulder and neck
- Shadow Boxing
    - o Rolling upper cuts in left and right stances

- o 4 Punch combination in left and right stances
- Knee lifts and Butt kicks
- At the end of this short period I want to have a light sweat starting to form. This means I have elevated my heart rate slightly and the blood has started to move around the body and warm the muscles up
- I now work through my Joint Dynamic Stretching as follows –
    - o Ankle twists 5 rotations each way on each ankle
    - o Knee rotations 5 rotations each way on each knee
    - o Hip joint rotations using Muay Thai inside and outside knee strike motion
    - o Lower back rotation with arms out and head facing forward
    - o Shoulder rotations forwards and backwards
    - o Neck rotations sideways, up and down, circles (critical this is slow and controlled!)
- I then move to Dynamic Stretching that is particular to the activity I am about to do. In this case let's assume its Kick Boxing –
    - o Front leg raises starting low and slowing getting higher
    - o Side leg raises starting low and slowly getting higher

- o Straight Knee strikes pushing hips forward
- o Various Elbow Strikes
- o Various punches
- I then finish my warm up with 1 minute of light and loose shadow sparring

This takes 5 minutes maximum depending on how cold it is or how you are feeling on the day. As I've said I can't stress enough how important the Warm-Up and the Warm-Down is as we get older. Be patient and take the time to do this. It will have enormous short term benefits to your existing injuries and joint limitations, but also major long terms benefits that will keep you training, fit and injury free for years to come.

BODY
The Sixth Step on the Journey....

Strength and Conditioning

As discussed earlier its important as we grow older to listen to our bodies, understand we can't do what we used to do when we were younger men, and accept and adapt. If we don't, we head down only one ultimate path where we continue to push through but we keep getting injured which leads to a continual 'recovery' mode of training, severe frustration…..…. and then we give up.

Do you want to let your ego keep you locked into training the 'Old Way' and end up doing nothing? Or do you want to be smart, adapt, and keep training in the future the *'Old Boys'* way?

Core Principals

The core principals around the Old Boys Strength and Conditioning program are –

- Focus is on major muscle groups –
    - Pectorals (Chest)
    - Latissimus (Lats/Back)
    - Triceps (Arms)
    - Biceps (Arms)
    - Abdominals (Core/Stomach)
    - Thighs (Legs)

- o   Hamstrings (Legs)
- o   Calves (Legs)
- Every workout focuses on a 'Whole of Body' approach which provides benefits to consistency and training times in a busy world
- One exercise per muscle group, per workout, is selected from a 'Menu' of exercise options
- Each exercise is completed for 5 sets, with a 15 second break between each set, with each set completed to failure
- Minimum reps for the 5 sets of one exercise is 50. If 50 reps cannot be completed in the 5 sets then the resistance should be reduced.
- Maximum reps for the 5 sets of one exercise is 100. If more than 100 reps can be completed in the 5 sets then the resistance should be increased.
- Routines and exercises are broken down to allow for the different situations we find ourselves in each day. We don't have time, we are travelling for work, we are away from home and don't have access to exercise equipment, or if we are able to access a fully equipped gym.

The Menu – Strength & Conditioning

As we've explained, the overall methodology of health and fitness revolves around the choice available from the 'Menu' system. The Strength and Conditioning Menu is based around the following core attributes –

- Select 1 exercise per body part from the Menu
- Complete each exercise for 5 sets with a 15 second break
- Sufficient resistance should be applied to keep total repetitions for the 5 sets in the 50-100 range

The 'Menu' or selection of exercises can be changed and added to, to suit your body type, existing injuries, or favourite exercises. But make sure you use the full menu over time and don't get caught up in one or two exercises. Constantly changing exercises keeps your muscles confused, helps prevent injury, and keeps motivation high.

An example of a Strength and Conditioning 'Menu' is as follows, but in summary understand that the Old Boy method aims to provide –

- Different workouts that can be selected, regardless of where you are, that will work with your available time, your current level of motivation, and your access to equipment or not. Anything, Anywhere, Anytime!

- The ability to select from multiple different exercises every day to combat boredom and to work around injuries and limitations

- A method of recording and maintaining consistency of your Health and Fitness Journey

Strength and Conditioning

Old Boys

The Menu – Strength & Conditioning

Exercise	Equipment	Resistance	Reps	Date
Chest				
Push-Ups Flat	Body Weight to Weight Vest	Body Weight	73	27.2.17
Push-ups Incline	Body Weight to Weight Vest			
Push-ups Decline	Body Weight to Weight Vest			
Dumbbell Flyes	Dumbbells			
Bench Press Flat	Barbell	40kg Barbell	62	2.3.17
Bench Press Incline				
Bench Press Decline	Barbell			
Butterfly Machine	Machine			
Double Punch	Resistance Band			
Back				
Seated Row	Machine	30kg	52	27.2.17
Lat Pull Down	Machine			
Single Dumbbell Rows	Dumbbells			
Bent over Rows	Barbell			
Seated Row	Resistance Band			
Bent Row	Resistance Band			
Abdominals				
Crunches				
Obliques				
Double Torso Curl				
Leg Raises				
Triceps				
Rope Push-Down	Machine	15kg	60	20.3.17
Dips Feet on Ground	Body Weight to Weight Vest	Body Weight	77	27.2.17
Dips Raised Legs	Body Weight to Weight Vest			
Overhead Rope Extension	Machine			
Ezy- Bar Extensions	Barbell			
Tricep Push-ups	Body Weight to Weight Vest			
Biceps				
Ezy-Bar Curl	Barbell			
Dumbbell Curls	Barbell			
Standing Curl	Resistance Band			
Thighs				
Squats	Body Weight to Weight Vest			
Single Leg Curl	Machine			
Double Leg Curl	Machine			
Hamstrings				
Single Leg Curl	Machine			
Double Leg Curl	Machine			
Roman Chair	Machine			
Deadlifts	Barbell			
Calves				
Calf Raises	Body Weight to Weight Vest			

BODY
The Seventh Step on the Journey....

Stamina and Aerobic Fitness

The first thing you often think when you start talking about getting back into some aerobic fitness is, let's go for a run. Now I personally hate running. I did a lot of it as a teenager and a young man and competed in athletics and middle distance running, but now I'd rather have my eyes poked out with a sharp stick.

Of course if you enjoy running (there could be something wrong with you) but get into it. What this is all about as we get older is finding some activity we get some enjoyment from that we can turn into a Stamina and Aerobic Fitness workout. Motivation to stay fit will not sustain you over the long term anymore so look for an activity, especially one where you can get involved with others, and use that as your commitment to aerobic fitness training.

Training with a group is especially helpful and creates motivation that you can never achieve on your own. As I mentioned in the introduction to this book, back in 2009 I started a group called *Old Boys Thai Boxing*. I had been involved in Martial Arts for a long time but as I neared 40 I really started to struggle training with and sparring the younger guys. Initially it was a mental thing being unable to accept that maybe I wasn't as quick or strong as I once was, then came the injuries, and then the lack of motivation. It was at this time I noticed a few guys my own age starting to drift away from the sport.

Over a beer I suggested to two of them we start doing some training on our own and push ourselves to our own limits, and spar to our own standards. They jumped at the opportunity to keep training in an environment that was ego free and so we started punching each other in the head two times a week. I'm still amazed the chord this has struck with Old Boys and where the club is today. We now have guys from all walks of life. It's not a fight club. Most of them have never thrown a punch in anger their entire lives, but they value two key things more than anything else they have ever done before –

1. Learning a fight skill that builds confidence
2. The camaraderie of a bunch of Old Boys who are all facing the same issues

The club has become something where the fitness and stamina component, whilst the key physical health benefit of the group, has become secondary to the sense of achievement and the camaraderie that it instils in guys who are at the Old Boy stage of life. I'm so very proud of what this club has become.

The point that this shows is that as we grow older we need to be engaged in a fitness routine that we enjoy, and that enjoyment does not necessarily have to come from the activity itself, but from the people we do it with.

Of course we can't always attend our fitness activity when we want. Our lives are busy, and just as we have created a choice of Strength and Conditioning routines to fit all situations, so to have I created a 'Menu' of Stamina based routines that can be utilised in all situations, at any time, in any place.

The Stamina Menu has the following categories -

- o **The Quickie**
- o **The Boxing Beep Test**
- o **12 Minute Burst**
- o **The Running Man**
- o **The Bag Man**
- o **Thai Boxing Circuit**
- o **Your Thing**

The Quickie

When you are time poor. You select one exercise from each of the Upper, Lower, and overall body categories. Each exercise is performed for 45 seconds, with a 15 second rest. Therefore each exercise takes 1 minute. Allow 5 minutes for Warm Up and 5 Minutes for warm down and then add as many 1 minute exercises as you have time available.

It can be easy when time poor to drop the warm up and warm down from the routine, but again I express how important and beneficial to long term joint and muscular health, that the warm up and down is.

The Boxing Beep Test

Takes the traditional running Beep Test and applies a Boxing or Kickboxing combination instead of running. How far can you get into the Beep test with that combination before you run out of steam? This also keeps a measure of your progress over time.

12 Minute Burst

This is a 12 minute whole of body routine developed specifically for Old Boys. It is 17 specific exercises covering the body from top to bottom. They are performed for 30 seconds with a 15 second break between each. Each exercise is weighted according to its complexity and level of effort required, then when repetitions are recorded they are automatically weighted and a final score is produced. This is an excellent measure and tracking of your progress.

The Running Man

This is a program aim at getting you back into a running routine or starting you on a running program. It however avoids long protracted running sessions that put consistent load on joints and especially knees. The Old Boys Running Man program is based on 4 minutes sets for 10 sets or a total of 40 minutes. The beginner starts at a 3 minute walk and 1 minute run for 5 sets and measures the distance they can travel. The distance travelled is built on and when the body and fitness allow this is slowly increased to 1 set of 2 minute walk and 2 minute run follow by the 4 sets of 1 and 3. The aim is to build up to 1 minute walk and 3 minute run for a full 10 sets. Once that level is achieved this is the maximum for maintenance and the focus becomes consistency of workout rather than increasing distance, time, or load.

The Bag Man

A series of Boxing and Muay Thai bag workouts that challenge you to learn and improve fight skills at the same time as improving your fitness and stamina.

Thai Boxing Circuit

A circuit of Boxing and Muay Thai skills that, like The Bag Man, also challenges you to learn and improve fight skills whilst improving fitness and stamina.

Your Thing

This can be anything. This is whatever you enjoy doing. It can be team sports, or mountain biking, or running or anything that you simply enjoy doing. I am a big believer in team sports the older we get. With team sports or group exercises, it's not just about the exercise, it's also about the motivation you get from working in a group, and also the camaraderie that comes from this, which in our very busy lives can be a great emotional support.

Some examples of these workouts follow at the end of this chapter.

The same philosophy is adopted for our Stamina workouts as was adopted for our strength program. The aims are threefold –

- Reduce overall workout time
- Reduce resistance on joints and tendons
- Increase Intensity by reducing intra set rest periods

On that basis many of the exercises can be adopted into the 5 set, 50-100 Rep, 15 second rest period, methodology that we have already explained. It makes the routines easy to remember and you can perform them anywhere, anytime.

In summary, the key lesson to take away from this section, in respect to working on your stamina and aerobic fitness, is to reduce the impact on joints and the body in general by reducing the resistance, but increasing the intensity by lowering rest times.....and if you can also find an activity that builds aerobic stamina, that can be done with a group, then that will help no end with your longer term motivation.

Old Boys
Stamina – The Quickie

How much time do you have?

- Allow 5 minutes for warm up
- Allow 1 minute per exercise (Select as many as time permits)
- Allow 5 minutes for warm down

Body Part	Exercise	Time	Rest	Reps	Date
Upper Body	Push-Ups Flat	45 sec	15 Sec		
	Push-ups Incline				
	Push-ups Decline				
	Tricep Dips				
	Boxing Combo				
	Shadow Sparring				
Lower Body	Jump Squats				
	Stair Run				
	Box Jumps				
	Kicking Combo				
Overall Body	Shuttle Run				
	Military Burpees				
	Bear Crawls				
	Battle Ropes				

Old Boys
Stamina – The Boxing Beep Test

- Select 1 combination for Beep Test

Combination	Level	Date
Jab, Cross, L/Hook, R/Body, L/Hook, R/Elbow, L/Knee, R/Knee	8.2	12.1.17
10 Right/Left Roundhouses	7.5	25.1.17
Jab, Cross, L/Hook, R/Elbow (5 sets)	9.5	15.2.17

Any kickboxing or boxing combination you want can be applied to the Boxing Beep Test

---

Old Boys
Stamina – The Bag Man

Combination

Switch L/Roundhouse, Cross, L/Hook

R/Uppercut, L/Hook, R/Elbow, L/Knee

Jab, Cross, L/Hook, R/Elbow, L/Knee

Any kickboxing or boxing combination you want can be applied to The Bag Man

- Select 1 Combination
- Warm Up
- 10 Sets of 45 Seconds each with 15 Second Rest
- 1 Burpee or Push-Up in Rest Period
- Warm Down

Old Boys
12 Minute Burst Tracker

Score	200	Work to be done
	300	On the move

Exercise	Time	Weighting	26.10.16 Reps	Score	Date Reps	Score	Date Reps	Score
Skipping	30 Sec	10%	60	6				
Flat Push-ups	30 sec	100%	23	23				
Bicep Curls Partner	30 sec	100%	10	10				
Tricep Dips	30 sec	100%	22	22				
Chinese Push-ups	30 sec	150%	6	9				
Skipping	30 sec	10%	30	3				
Crunches	30 sec	100%	22	22				
Oblique Left	30 sec	100%	12	12				
Oblique Right	30 sec	100%	12	12				
Double Torso	30 sec	150%	25	38				
Leg Raises	30 sec	150%	15	23				
Elbow/Knee Doubles	30 sec	100%	26	26				
Skipping	30 sec	10%	24	2				
Knee Lifts	30 sec	50%	26		13			
Skipping	30 sec	10%	30		3			
Military Burpees	30 sec	500%	7		35			
Skipping	30 sec	10%	26		3			
Total	**12 min**				262			

Old Boys
Stamina – The Running Man

	Goal	Actual 5.4.16	Actual 20.5.16	Actual 15.6.16	Actual 10.7.16
Run	3 min	1 min	1 min	1 min	2 min
Rest	1 min	3 min	3 min	3 min	2 min
Sets	10	5	7	10	5
Distance	6km	1.5km	2.37km	3.10km	2.90km

Run Avg Pace   10km/hr
Walk Avg Pace   5km/hr

Old Boys
Stamina – Old Boys Thai Boxing Skills

- Select 1 combination per station
- As many stations as time permits
- Warm up and Warm down

Combination	Set Time	Rest Time
Switch L/Roundhouse, Cross, L/Hook	45 sec	15 sec
R/Uppercut, L/Hook, R/Elbow, L/Knee		
Jab, Cross, L/Hook, R/Elbow, L/Knee		
Jab, Cross, R/Roundhouse		
…….etc.		

Any kickboxing or boxing combination you want can be applied to The Circuit

Old Boys
Stamina – Your Thing

This is your activity that you enjoy. It could be anything including but far from limited to –
- Old Boys Thai Boxing
- Boxing Training
- Touch Football
- Running
- Bike Riding
- Beach Volleyball
- Indoor Cricket
- Etc. etc. etc.

BODY
The Eighth Step on the Journey....

Flexibility, Warm Down, Yoga

As important as the warm-up is, so too is the warm down. You've heard all your life how important it is to warm up and warm down, but it's only as we get a little older and there are some aching joints and muscles that take twice as long to recover from, that we see the real benefit of this.

There are 3 clear components to this step that I believe should be addressed –

1. **Warm Down** – At the end of a workout our muscles are loose and full of blood. This is the time we want to complete some static stretching. Doing static stretching when the muscles are warm will help set the muscles neuro sensors to a greater stretch and helps prevent injury. It also helps with existing injuries, by holding a stretch in a static position, just a fraction beyond your comfort zone, and relaxing into the stretch and breathing through for at least 30 seconds, can help in overall muscle recovery from a workout.

2. **Flexibility** – This is not about doing the splits (although if you can do that then great) but it's about range of movement in joints, tendons and muscles. Maintaining a greater range of motion is one of the best injury preventers you can do.

3. **Yoga** – When I trained Muay Thai in Thailand, all the professional fighters (I wasn't a professional fighter… ..I just hid in the back and did the yoga class) were required to do an hours supervised Yoga session every morning. I can tell you from firsthand experience that after only 2 weeks of this, my flexibility and recovery was improved significantly. But it's not just the physical benefits that I was impressed with, it was the emotional impacts on stress and anxiety that I was most amazed with. I know many middle aged men scoff at Yoga as some sort of yuppie trend, but if it's good enough for some of Thailand's best Muay Thai professionals….it's good enough for the average Joe!

It's a Journey of Self Discovery

I can't stress enough that the *Old Boys Health and Fitness System* is about self-discovery. It's about taking a good hard honest look at yourself, your strengths and limitations, and building a routine that works for you physically and mentally.

Yes we provide a framework for Strength, Stamina, and Flexibility, within which we suggest a methodology to training as you get older, but none of this means you are restricted to the exercises presented here. What it provides is a framework (types of routines depending on your circumstances – stop making excuses not to train) and a theory of training (lower resistance, lower rest) that you can adjust with whatever exercise you choose or activities that you like to do.

An example of a Warm Down and Yoga routine is as follows.

Flexibility, Warm Down, Yoga

Old Boys
Warm Down

The Quickie - 5 minutes

| **Stretch** | **Comment** |

Touch Toes
Back on Calves
Back on knees, knees apart
Slide through and arch up
Hip flexors
On back knees either side
Reverse arch

Yoga – 20-30 minutes

- All stretches/poses are held for 3 breaths. In and out is 1 breath

Body Stretch
- Flat on back, hands above head, stretch out body
- Relax on back, 3 circular breaths
-

Neck
- Nose to armpit
- Left and right static
-

Shoulders
- Arm up and behind against wall
- Arm up and hand down behind shoulder blades
-

Core
- Touch toes
- Walk forward an back on calves
- Raise each leg up and hold
- Turn to side and 1 arm pointing to sky – both sides
- Onto knees with knees out wide then down onto elbows
- Slide through and arch up
- Cat Stretches
-

Standing Poses
- Half Lotus one leg
- Warrior pose
-

Hips
- Hip Flexor Stretch
- Lead leg across body
- The 'Rusty'
-

Hamstrings
- Toe touch
- Front splits
- Side splits
-

Lower Back
- Bridge from back
- Knees up and to either side look opposite way
- Reverse Arch
-

Body Stretch
- Flat on back, hands above head, stretch out body
-

Meditation

BODY
The Ninth Step on the Journey....

Nutrition, Diet and Supplements

Nutrition, weight loss, diet management, counting calories, weighing food, can't eat this, must eat that....... **STOP!!**

It's hard enough as we get older to have the mental space let alone time, to commit to counting calories and watching everything we eat. What we need is a simplistic approach that offers a manageable method of diet control, and most importantly one that is maintainable mentally....and by that I mean committing to a healthy diet that does not completely cut out our little vices.

The *Old Boys Nutrition Methodology* is all about the KISS principal, Keep It Simple Stupid. Some basic nutritional facts and practices applied in a manageable way every day, with the aim that small improvements become part of our everyday life.

This section could be an entire book on its own (and there are countless books out there on this topic) but for us Old Boys it's all about understanding and monitoring of your current diet, its flaws, and how to start setting a new direction for your dietary intake that will improve weight control, energy levels, and overall health.

I really hate counting calories, but this doesn't mean you can't get enthusiastic and keep track of your calories in detail, and there are many Apps out there that will do that for you. But personally I get bored with this after the first day.....and I like chocolate too much. As we get older, and we are not training for a specific challenge, but are just wanting to maintain a healthy lifestyle, the motivation to count calories and be ultra-strict on our diets is a very difficult thing to maintain. Hence our KISS methodology and providing yourself with a basic understanding, that when coupled with a little self-awareness, can make an enormous difference to your overall health.

Our methodology covers the following key elements -

- Food types and nutritional content
- Portion Control
- Diet Planning
- 'Vice' Recognition and Monitoring
- Supplements

Food Types and Nutritional Content

Whilst it is not essential to be an expert on all the different types of food, contents, impacts on blood sugar etc., it is important to have a basic knowledge of some key items so that you know what to look for and so that you can become aware of what you are eating.

Carbohydrates – Are our fuel. They are the foods that give us energy. There are two types of Carbs being Simple and Complex. Simple Carbs are easily broken down and provide a quick short term energy boost. Simple Carbs are often found in refined foods but also include foods such as –

o Fruit
o Sugar

- o White Flour
- o Soft Drinks
- o Cakes
- o Cookies

Complex Carbs and slow release carbs provide lasting energy throughout a working day and through workouts. They importantly include fibre and starch and include food groups such as –

- o Pasta
- o Potatoes
- o Rice
- o Grains

Carbs are important to start the day and during the day to assist with maintenance of energy levels, but should be minimised at the end of the day before sleeping.

Protein – Is the building blocks of our body and builds muscle, works to fix injuries, and generally keeps our bodies solid and strong. Protein is the most well marketed supplement around and has made more people rich from distribution and selling, than it has built muscle. Whilst Protein is important for muscle growth and recovery, it's important to note that the recommended minimum daily requirement for an adult is one gram per kilogram of bodyweight. Sellers and distributors of Protein supplements will suggest 3 to 4 times that amount if you want to make gains, but unless you are an elite level athlete, the recommended allowance is really all you need.

Excess Protein can be turned straight into body fat, so be careful. Also protein cannot be stored in the body for use at a later date, so it requires small consistent intake rather than large inconsistence quantities.

Proteins are included in food groups such as –

- o Milk
- o Eggs
- o Chicken
- o Red Meat
- o Beans

Fats – Fats….BAD. Well that's what immediately comes to mind and the market place tells us that constantly. But as with most things in life there is an element of truth and an element of good quality marketing (fiction) in this statement. There are two types of fats to be aware of-

1. Unsaturated
    a. Polyunsaturated
    b. Monounsaturated
2. Saturated

Polyunsaturated fats like Omega 3 from fish, and Monounsaturated fats from vegetable sources including Olive Oil, Avocados, and Almonds etc. are a vital component in your diet. They are necessary for the health and function of your nerves, skin and hair, and for the transportation of vitamins A, D, E and K around the body.

Saturated fats found in processed foods such as Pizza, Cheese, and Dairy Deserts provide little value to the body. They provide some level of taste but they also contain more than twice as many calories per gram than either protein or carbohydrates.

Fibre – Fibre is roughage. It is a component of everyone's diet that provides no nutritional value what so ever as it is indigestible. But dietary fibre is essential to our inner health and to a functional working of our digestive system. This is because it helps to promote bowel regularity because fibre absorbs water in the intestines, and avoids constipation. Fibre in your diet also speeds up the elimination of toxins through the bowels and a high fibre diet can halve the amount of time it takes food to transit your entire digestive tract. Importantly fibre makes you feel fuller quicker and longer so it assists with reducing the intake of overall calories.

Fibre is found in found groups such as –

- o Bran cereal
- o Grain bread
- o Fresh vegetables
- o Fresh fruits
- o Salad greens
- o Nuts and seeds

Sugar

Sugar is one of modern society's biggest nutritional issues. Sugar is utilised in manufactured foods to add taste and bulk.

It is an addictive substance and has the ability to cause all manner of health issues.

But again there is good and bad in this issue. Sugar can be broadly split into 2 types –

1. Natural
2. Added

Natural sugars are called simple sugars and are found in fruit, vegetables, beans, nuts and whole grains among other things. When contained in whole foods they come with vitamins, minerals, protein, phytochemicals and fibre. The presence of fibre makes a significant difference because it slows down the absorption of sugar, which moderates its impact on blood sugar levels. Natural sugar in whole foods is good sugar.

Added sugars are refined sugars that is added during the processing, cooking, or manufacturing process. When you consume these refined added sugars you consume calories without any nutrients or fibre content. Added sugar is bad sugar. The obvious culprits are soft drinks and lollies, but also be very careful of breakfast cereals with dried fruit and nuts, that market themselves as healthy choices. These often contain large amounts of added refined sugars.

Bad sugars increase your risk of weight gain, and developing Type 2 diabetes and heart disease. One teaspoon of sugar has 16 calories. You'll get 8 teaspoons of sugar from a can of soft drink. When sugar enters your bloodstream, your pancreas releases insulin, which enables sugar to move into cells. Sometimes, with too much sugar, your cells can become resistant to insulin which means the sugar stays in your blood and increases your risk of Type 2 Diabetes or heart disease.

There is an excellent documentary on sugar that you should all take the time to view. It is called 'That Sugar Film' and has been produced by an Australian Damon Gameua. It really explains society's addiction to sugar and how it is impacting our lives.

Calorie Counting

Whilst we've said our approach to diet and nutrition does not involve micro managing your calorie count on a daily basis, it is important to understand what calories are, what foods are good and bad, and how many calories per day is healthy intake.

Calories are a measure of the energy in foods. As discussed above there are good and bad types of the same food, so therefore there are good and bad caloric intake. 1,000 calories ingested from fresh fruit and vegetables is not the same as 1,000 calories ingested from ice-cream. A simple and obvious statement you say……yes, but have a good hard look at your diet. You know where the bad calories are, but what do you actually do about it? It's very easy to talk a good game, but very hard to walk the talk, when it comes to diet and caloric intake, and I say this from my own ongoing experience with chocolate.

As we continually say, the Old Boys method is about a journey of self-discovery, not blindly following a set diet that is marketed to you on the basis it will turn you into a lean muscle machine in 6 weeks! Educate yourself, understand your lifestyle, be realistic about your goals, and take small steps towards a longer term goal………..and don't make excuses.

An individual's daily caloric intake can vary significantly depending on –

- o Age
- o Weight
- o Type of Work
- o Physical Activity

But as a guide the following table sets out some rough parameters for caloric intake per day, required to maintain weight. But I encourage you to research and learn for yourself what works for you.

Weight	Activity Level	Calories per Day
80kg	Sedentary	2,000
	Moderately Active	2,200
	Active	2,400
90kg	Sedentary	2,200
	Moderately Active	2,400
	Active	2,600
100kg	Sedentary	2,400
	Moderately Active	2,600
	Active	2,800

But it is not Rocket Science and there are 4 simple rules –

1. If you want to lose weight you need to burn more calories through activity than you ingest

2. If you want to gain weight you need to ingest more calories than you burn

3. Keep the gap between burnt calories and calories ingested on a daily basis small, don't go for massive weight loss and weight gain. This is difficult to maintain in the long term, and can be unhealthy. Gradual progression is the key.

4. Make sure the calories you ingest are 'good' calories not 'bad' ones

Portion Control

This is the biggest mistake we all make. The size of our meals. Whilst many of us may well eat reasonably healthy meals the majority of the time, it is the size of each portion that is killing western society. If you take nothing else out of this chapter, take this one component and have a good hard look at your portion sizes.

What is a Portion size? Generally speaking a portion of food is the size of the palm of your hand. It's not a scientific measurement, but let's face it, if it gets too complex we lose interest.

Generally if a meal consists of a portion of Protein, a portion of Good Carbs, and a portion of vegetables or greens, then you are on the right track. We always eat until we are full, rather than eat until we are sustained. It sounds simple but portion control is one of the hardest diet control tools you will have to master, but it is in my opinion the most important.

Diet Planning

Diet planning sounds like a laborious task akin to watching paint dry, and you can easily turn it into that if you want. But there are a few simple rules and actions that if you take the time to set up, can make this an activity that will not only be great for your diet and health, but will add hours to your week. This is the part of the equation that most people don't give credit to…the time saved during the week due to reduced meal prep time. Having a pre-prepared diet also prevents that easy out of the Macca's run, when you're too busy.

The key rules for Old Boys Diet Planning are –

1. **Eat 4 or 5 smaller meals a day instead of 3 big meals a day**

Smaller more frequent meals keep your energy levels at a better balance throughout the day and give you better physical and mental function. Having 2 or 3 big meals spaced out can see large ups and downs in blood sugar and general energy levels that impact on your ability to perform.

Also by having smaller more frequent meals during the day means your metabolism is working all the time and when your metabolism is working you are burning calories. So it actually helps with weight control.

Personally my routine is a good breakfast about 7am, a meal at about 11am, a meal at about 3pm, and then dinner at about 8pm. Work out what works best for you but try and keep the meals spaced as regularly as your lifestyle will allow.

2. **Ratio of Carbohydrates, Proteins and Fats**

Generally speaking try and have a portion of Carbs, Protein, and good Fats with every meal, in acceptable portions sizes. If you want to get a little more technical then your breakfast and meals 2 and 3 may be a little more weighted towards carbs for energy and meals 4 and dinner may become a little more weighted towards protein. The key with your last meal before sleeping is to make it your smallest meal as it will sit in your stomach over night when the body is at its lowest ebb for burning calories. This of course is a real change of lifestyle for most of us as Dinner has become the main meal in our lives. If nothing else keep a real close eye on your portions sizes at night time.

3. Raw Foods not Processed

Always aim to have your nutrition come from the least processed food possible. Things such as steak and vegetables and salads are examples of Raw Foods and contain all the good protein, carbs, fat and sugars. The more a food is processed the more external additives are involved and the lower the nutritional value becomes. Remember the food industry is built on creating additives that enhance taste and hence enhance our desire for that food and of course we then eat more of it and buy more of it.

This isn't to say you give up chocolate or hotdogs, (chocolate is a staple for me), it just means be aware of what you are eating, and when you get the choice, go with the lowest processed option.

4. Make it easy - Pre-Prep meals

This is such an effective action to take. Whilst it may take an hour or two on a weekend, if you pre-prepare your meals and package them up for the week, your ability to stay on track with your diet will be increased ten-fold, and the time you save in your day will be amazing.

'Vice' Recognition and Monitoring

This is a practice I highly recommend. It's all part of this journey of self-discovery and being honest with yourself. We all have 'Vices' including such things as Coffee, Chocolate, Wine, Beer, Smoking etc. There are many different methods available for dealing with your addictions, but the Old Boys method of dealing with addictions and vices, is all about self-awareness, taking achievable consistent action, and managing change.

I'm not generally in favour of the 'Cold Turkey' approach. Going cold turkey is not a long term solution for legal vices (I'm not commenting on drugs or illegal substances). Our program is about recognising our vices and acknowledging the impact they have long term, then making small changes that lead to long term lifestyle changes. But I have to self-disclose here, ever since my Boarding School days I have had a complete and uncontrollable addiction to Milo. I tried for years to convince myself it was the Food of Champions like it says on the tin, and it does have certain nutritional value, but not in the quantities I can eat Milo….. So the only solution for me is to not have it in the house. Sometimes you just have to cut the cord……

TASK:

Take the time to go to your quite, not to be disturbed place. It's important you take a very non-emotional and non-judgemental perspective in this process. List every single thing that passes your lips over the course of a week, then with the knowledge you have gained to this point, identify what elements are not providing nutritional value and recognise what vices and addictions you may have. Brainstorm them all down.

A suggestion is to do this process after you have eaten a meal and are full. Being hungry can cloud your judgement when trying to identify vices that are no good for you. Because you are hungry you will look for excuses as to why it's not really a problem! Believe me it's the same rule as don't go shopping when you're hungry.

Once you have identified all your Vices and their quantities, work through some easily achievable targets you could do right now to reduce the impact of these issues. Don't be a hero and say I will stop smoking or drinking as of tomorrow morning. It won't be sustainable. Baby steps boys! It can be as simple as one less beer a day or 2 less cigarettes a day. Make it achievable. What the key part is, is to make yourself accountable and monitor your progress. Keep to the small goals for a minimum of 21 days, and then review and shift the goal a little further. Getting your emotional system used to the changes by keeping the changes small and achievable, but consistent, is the key to long term sustainability.

Supplements

The supplement industry has grown exponentially over the last decade. Where once supplements were the domain of the elite athlete, now even the week-end warrior takes at least a protein powder.

As with any product in any industry, the vast majority of the growth is purely and simply excellent marketing. Protein is the greatest source of amazement for me although pre and post workout formulas come a close second. What we need to understand is that as a week-end warrior, if we eat generally healthy (remember good carbs, natural sugars, and non-processed foods?) we can get the majority of the vitamins, minerals, amino acids, and all other sorts of supplements, from the foods we eat every day.

However not all the hype is pure marketing and there is room for key supplements, in acceptable quantities at correct times. The role of supplements as we grow older should be of a higher priority. There are 3 key supplements that should be considered a daily essential for *Old Boys* -

- A Protein Supplement
- A Joint Health formula
- A Multi-vitamin

The Protein supplement helps with repair and recovery of the body after physical activity.

The Joint Formula helps with the aging process and assists with keeping our joints and tendons lubricated and flexible.

A multi-vitamin assists with general health and keeps the body's level of essential vitamins and minerals in balance. This assists the immune system do its job.

Quantity is a key, especially as it relates to protein supplements. The industry as a generalisation, tends to suggest we need more protein than we really do, but it's not completely false advertising. What they suggest is that you are a hard working athlete, you train hard and want to recover quickly to train hard again. However there is a difference between how hard we think we train and how hard we actually train. There is actually a psychological symptom that some people have where they think the more protein they take the harder they must be working! The supplement companies love these people. You need to be open and transparent with yourself about how hard you work, understand what supplements you are getting from the diet you already have, how can you improve that intake through diet, and then what's left between the improved diet and how hard you train is what level of supplementation you need. Stop wasting money on supplements that are providing no discernible nutritional value, and may in fact be simply adding weight to the scales and reducing weight from your wallet!

The other key element is timing. An example in simple terms would be - don't eat lots of carbs before you go to bed as they will just sit in your stomach and be slowly digested and the energy value will be lost. Think about when you need energy, when will the body best repair itself, and work with those simple guidelines when planning your supplementation.

TASK:

Review the last week. Be very detailed. Record everything that you have ingested. Now do some research on the nutritional values of what you have ingested (there are many excellent apps for this. I have used 'My Fitness Pal' which is a great app for understanding the components of your diet).

Now take a long hard look at your current diet and see whether you can make improvements that will increase or decrease proteins, carbs, fats, sugars, whatever fits with your health and fitness goals. Understand what calories you are now consuming.

Now record every bit of physical activity you engaged in during the week. This is not just specific training but can include work especially if you have a physically demanding job. Research how many calories you may burn during a standard week. Again there are many apps available for this.

Now you have a new and improved diet and an understanding of your physical activity and your calories burnt. Are you in deficit or are you over suppling your body? If you're low on energy at certain times of the day you may want to supplement some calories with extra good carbs earlier in the day. If you're finding it hard to recover from a day's work and an exercise regime then you may consider supplementing your protein intake. Again I reiterate this is a journey of discovery about yourself, how your body works, and what you can do to be the best example of who you could possibly be. If you do the research and discover for yourself, your motivation to stay the course takes a strong bump in the right direction.

BODY
The Tenth Step on the Journey....

Tracking and Measuring Progress

Tracking and measuring progress seems to be an obvious thing to do to ensure improvement of overall health and fitness, and it is. HOWEVER for Old Boys it can be a double edged sword. The reason is that as Old Boys, one of the problems we have noticed is that we can't lift the weights we used to, run the distances we used to, recover from injuries like we used to. As such it can be easy for tracking and recording to become an emotional liability that highlights your inability to consistently improve. Remember earlier we spoke about the need to accept your limitations, but do not be defined by them? If you do not accept your limitations through injury or other, and you have the mindset of Break or Break Through, then you will be disappointed when you reach a level of health and fitness only to get injured and lose the gains made because it takes you so long to recover these days.

I'm not talking to high level athletes here, and you probably know what you're doing anyway, but I am talking to the Old Boy who was once an active athlete and who is getting back into it to improve their physical self. You in particular need to be careful. Your mindset is everything. Yes, have a goal to reach, but understand that this is a journey of improvement and then maintenance of that standard over the long-

> *Accept your physical limitations, but be careful you don't use them as an excuse. There is a difference.*
>
> **JR**

er term……you will never be the 20 year old elite athlete you once where!! Accept that….but DO NOT use that as an excuse and accept something less than what you can be.

So having said that, I will say that tracking and measuring is still a very useful tool. Sounds a bit contradictory but it's how you use the information that tracking and measuring highlights that is the key, not the actual progress.

Especially when starting off on the journey of getting your physical health back on track, setting a goal, then recording where you are when you start, then recording your progress, can be the most motivational tool you can use. You see improvements quickly and that in itself gets you up and attacking the next session.

It's when you get to the physical level that is nearing the best you can be within your physical limitations that progress slows and tracking and measuring can lose its lustre. **At this stage change your thinking from regular tracking of your improvement, to tracking your consistency of workout, your level of injury, and use the information to make sure you are staying on track, and pushing hard, or highlight when you are not trying hard enough.**

There is no right or wrong way to track and measure, but what follows are some of the systems I have developed and have found to be very useful.

Stamina – The 12 Minute Burst

The 12 Minute Burst is a series of exercises selected to work the whole body, in an intense anaerobic state. The routine is structured such that it can be done by anyone at any level, with results tracked and recorded, and measured against past performance to reflect improvements.

Each exercise has a particular 'weighting' considering its level of technical or physical difficulty. The lower the weighting the easier the exercise and hence the more you should be able to do in the set time. The higher the weighting the harder the exercise and with more difficulty comes less repetitions in the set time.

Each exercise is performed for 30 seconds, followed by a 15 second break in which time you record the reps you completed of that exercise. This continues for 12 minutes through all the exercises.

The 12 Minute Burst Tracker comes in a simple spreadsheet format where on completion the repetitions performed against each exercise are entered and they automatically add up against the relevant 'weighting' and provide a final overall score. It's this score that is then compared to past workouts and to future workouts to track how you are progressing.

The scoring system reflects the following outcomes –

Score	Comment
200	Work to be done
300	On the move
400	Good
500	Excellent
600	Nice Work Old Boy

Following is an example 12 Minute Burst Tracker from one of my clients. This Old Boy is 40 years of age, has been inactive for about 15 years since giving away Footy and has been working hard and raising a family, and physical fitness has been a poor second to everything else. He's at that stage he wants to get some life back and he took up the challenge. You'll see how his results started very low and that was a real shock for him, he actually didn't even finish, but that is ok, that is the base line. He knew where he was and once the initial shock disappeared he had a goal to reach 400.

Remember this is a tool to record and should be used no more than once a week as a workout that fits into your overall training routine. Don't record your results any more than once a week, in fact I suggest only record every two weeks. Allow your body time to improve through your overall training routine and see bigger changes over time.

The Boxing Beep Test

Another method of stamina tracking I have developed is the **Boxing Beep Test**. This takes the traditional running Beep Test and applies a Boxing or Kickboxing combination instead of running. The aim is to learn and practice boxing and kickboxing skills whilst working your fitness levels.

You work that set combination once for each lap, just as you would run one lap in a standard Beep Test. How far can you get onto the Beep Test with that combination before you run out of steam? Record your result and try to beat it next time.

The combination can be altered at any time for any reason but make sure you compare scores against the same combination. You may have several different combination comparisons running over time, just to keep things fresh.

Old Boys
12 Minute Burst Tracker

Score 200 Work to be done
      300 On the move

Exercise	Time	Weighting	2.8.16 Reps	Score	24.10.16 Reps	Score	10.12.16 Reps	Score
Skipping	30 Sec	10%	60	6	70	7	85	9
Flat Push-ups	30 sec	100%	23	23	24	24	35	35
Bicep Curls Partner	30 sec	100%	10	10	15	15	21	21
Tricep Dips	30 sec	100%	22	22	26	26	39	39
Chinese Push-ups	30 sec	150%	6	9	8	12	12	18
Skipping	30 sec	10%	30	3	55	6	70	7
Crunches	30 sec	100%	22	22	30	30	35	35
Oblique Left	30 sec	100%	12	12	20	20	30	30
Oblique Right	30 sec	100%	12	12	20	20	30	30
Double Torso	30 sec	150%	25	38	25	38	32	48
Leg Raises	30 sec	150%	15	23	25	38	30	45
Elbow/Knee Doubles	30 sec	100%	0	0	35	35	42	42
Skipping	30 sec	10%	24	2	30	3	40	4
Knee Lifts	30 sec	50%	26	13	35	18	40	20
Skipping	30 sec	10%	30	3	30	3	35	4
Military Burpees	30 sec	500%	1	5	8	40	10	50
Skipping	30 sec	10%	26	3	25	3	35	4
Total	**12 min**	**208**		**341**				**445**

Strength and Conditioning Tracking

The same principals of tracking and recording apply to strength and conditioning tracking as well as stamina. Tracking and recording progress in the early phases of getting your life back under control is extremely valuable and will help motivate you and keep you focused on the goal ahead, however the closer you get to your goal, that is a factor of your age and limitations, the slower the progress will become. As discussed above, at this stage it is critical that tracking and recording becomes a long term maintenance to check you are maintaining a level of strength rather than looking to break records each week.

Remember this workout routine is designed to be changed and used by you to include exercises that work for you. It's the methodology that's important, not the types of exercises. Work with whatever exercises work best for your body and its strengths or limitations.

Repetitions and Your Favourite Playlist

If there is one thing that helped me come to grips with maintaining a level of fitness rather than trying to improve every workout, was to stop counting my repetitions. As a habit I always counted reps and was always comparing to the last workout. As I got older this just became depressing as I wasn't improving and sometimes falling behind if I hadn't worked out for a week because I was busy at work or with family. It's such a small change but I did two things at the same time that took away this level of frustration.

1. I downloaded all my old favourite 80's music and created playlists

2. I stopped counting reps and started listening to music

Now instead of counting reps I listen to my music and I refuse to count reps. I do each set to failure but the whole set I am rocking out to ACDC or Midnight Oil (or the Village People but I don't tell anyone about that). It makes the workout so much more enjoyable and I am not constantly comparing myself to who I was last week.

I still do record my reps to see if I am on track but I do it only once per month now instead of every session. Give it a go, I guarantee it will make a difference.

Nutrition and Weight Tracking

This is where things can get very daunting, and can easily get out of hand. By this I mean that there are countless different Apps and methods available to track your nutritional intake, and more than enough people to give you advice on the calories and nutritional value of foods. You can make tracking nutritional intake as complex as you want.

But let's face it, that's just boring. As Old Boys we have some vices, we enjoy a beer or a nice wine, and personally I'm a big fan of chocolate (and I may have mentioned Milo).

The key is moderation.

Now you may have set yourself a challenging goal and be training for a specific event like a triathlon or similar, and at these times then you definitely set some strict diet goals and track the nutritional value of your foods. With a specific and date constrained goal in mind, the motivation can be sustained to maintain a strict diet plan. However what I am more specifically focused on is the day to day living. For us it's all about maintaining a sensible diet, with our vices or pleasurable foods in moderation. Portion size as we've discussed is I believe one of the keys.

In the same vain as the tracking and recording of Stamina and Strength, I find it very useful for a week to actually do a detailed tracking of everything that I ingest. 'My Fitness Pal' is an excellent free App that can help you with this process. By recording for one week, and breaking down the nutritional value of all the foods you consume, you will very quickly highlight where you are in terms of Proteins, Carbs, Fats, and general caloric intake against your lifestyle and caloric output through exercise and physical activity. At the end of week one sit down and adjust your diet to bring it more into line with the principals we've discussed in this chapter, and more in line with your lifestyle. Then for the next week record everything again and see how you have improved and where your weaknesses are. This 2 week process will provide you with an invaluable insight into your eating habits that you currently do almost subconsciously, or that you believe are healthy and actually turn out not to be.

Once you have completed the Vice Recognition process plus the 2 week Nutritional Adjustment as described above, you will have a solid foundation for a balanced diet. It's important however to come back and review where you are at by repeating the same process of Vice Recognition and 2 week Nutritional Adjustment, on a regular basis. For some it may be monthly for others it may be 6 monthly, but don't kid yourself that you are going well because it's so easy to slip back into old habits. Personally I recommend doing this exercise every 3 months.

Tracking of Weight gain or loss is something that many people see as the most important element to track, but in reality this is because it is the easiest. Tracking your weight gain or loss can be fraught with physical and emotional dangers if you are not aware. For many men gaining weight when you are in the process of a good weights program can be seen as a good thing. Muscle is heavier than fat right? But as we get older that could simply be that because you are working harder you are eating more and your control of Portion Sizes has become lost. But you need more calories to train harder right? Be very careful you are not fooling yourself. Weight gain must be lean muscle, not fat through a positive caloric intake.

With weight loss, I don't recommend fast weight loss or fad diets. The Old Boys system is all about creating a long term sustainable program of overall health that gets great results over the longer term, not short term wins that are not sustainable.

When tracking weight gain or loss, try and keep it to one day a week, the same day, and at the same time. Your weight can vary dramatically dependent on the time of day, your hydration, and your current health. But the real key is not to get hung up on your weight. It is a single small tool, in a large tool box full of ways to track and monitor your overall health and fitness, so treat it as such.

The **Visual Tool** is one of those things that either gets overlooked or distorted, yet can be one of the most motivating. Simply looking at yourself in the mirror and comparing week to week can be a very strong method of tracking, if you can separate self-judgement from reality. Don't be critical of yourself, just be realistic. Take a series of photos as well to compare your progress, but taking selfies and posting to Facebook……. Don't be that guy! Remember if this Health and Fitness trip is about you receiving praise and the thumbs up from others on social media, then you're doing it for all the wrong reasons. Us Old Boys are at that stage of life where we are doing all this for ourselves and our close loved ones. If you can't take this life changing journey for yourself, you certainly won't stay motivated waiting for others to tell you how great you are.

BODY
The Eleventh Step on the Journey....

Motivation

Staying the Course

This is the hard part isn't it? How do we maintain our motivation for the long term? How do we make this a lifestyle, and not a daily chore? Contrary to popular belief it has nothing to do with keeping your eye on the prize, fighting hard, chasing the dream, watching motivational videos, or telling yourself you are a strong and confident person every morning. All these things, despite what the internet and motivational videos will tell you, make your journey no easier and in fact can make it significantly harder.

But how could these positive actions actually make staying the course harder? Well it all comes down to our Attitude. External motivating factors mean absolutely nothing if your attitude is not tuned in, and in fact will leave you feeling deflated that you can't follow through after listening to that motivational video.

Attitude

What do I mean by attitude when it comes to physical health? Isn't being positive and doing all those positive things, a way of adopting a positive attitude? Well yes it is but…..when I talk about attitude I mean a deeper internal aspect of your personality that is built across the 4 Pillars of your life (remember those - Mind, Body, Soul, Living). External motivating factors such as positive affirmations and posting motivational sayings on Facebook will mean absolutely nothing if your internal attitude is not set right.

Attitude, as we discussed in the MIND chapter, encompasses your Values, your Belief Systems, understanding your Core Beliefs and your subsequent Automatic Thoughts and how they impact your actions.

This whole journey is about understanding your attitude and becoming aware of your thoughts and actions. Through awareness of who you really are, comes a sense of acceptance and calm.

Your Values and Belief systems we discussed in detail in the Mind Journey are the core intangible reasons you do what you do, why you get up in the morning, and what you want your life story to be.

It's important in this process to understand your Core Beliefs as well. Core beliefs are beliefs and attitudes that we have built up over our lifetime of experiences and have become so entrenched that we are unconscious of them. From Core Beliefs come Automatic Thoughts and with Automatic Thoughts come Automatic Behaviours. For example you may have had a bad experience with a car salesman when you were younger, you bought a car and it turned out to be a lemon. From that you have developed a Core Belief that all car salesman are out to rip you off. When you see a car salesman you immediately think and feel distrust, which subsequently makes you act in a certain way that is generally negative. This negative reaction then reinforces the core belief and so the circle goes on, despite the fact nothing at all may have happened the last time you saw a car salesman.

If through this Journey you are able to identify these Core Beliefs and understand how they run counterproductive to your true Values and what you want your life story to be, then this is what will provide rock solid motivation to stay the course. Being aware of yourself, your thoughts and reactions, and how that impacts your goals, is like laying down a deep concrete footing on which you can build your Life. It's not fool proof as there are many things outside your control that can topple your structure, but with a solid foundation you can easily rebuild.

Adjusting the Rudder

We've spoken before about being able to adjust the rudder and change direction as you move forward. The worst thing you can do is to get stuck on a workout or dietary plan with no changes or adjustments. The impacts are two fold –

1. If you continue to do the same exercises all the time your body will adjust and gains will slowly stop until they start to become losses. You must change exercise types to keep your nervous system and muscles from locking into a set routine. Also by working your muscles and joints from many different angles will help prevent injuries in the long term.

2. Doing the same thing all the time is like watching paint dry. Make changes in your workouts and diet to keep things fresh and interesting.

Adjusting the rudder doesn't just have to mean the actual types of exercise you do, it can also refer

Motivation is a journey of attitude, adjustment and acceptance.

JR

to intensity. Some days you just can't face pushing yourself hard, so on those days drop the intensity to 50%. Don't even go near your muscle failure point. You will be amazed how good you feel having done a 50% intensity workout and barely broken a sweat, compared to having done nothing and sat in front of the TV.

Acceptance – Cut yourself some slack

Things get in the way. Work, injury, family, life in general. Make exercise a thing you do consistently over the long term. Don't get hung up on doing 4 workouts a week and if you only do one this week you have failed and you have to do 6 next week to make up for it.

Cut yourself some slack, but be aware when you start using 'life' as an excuse for just being a lazy bastard though. Cutting yourself some slack is not an excuse to not do a low intensity short workout.

The older we get the easier it is to do nothing, but you will pay for it in the long term both physically and mentally, as your joints begin to seize up, and you start to beat yourself up because you wish you had kept your fitness up.

BODY
The Twelfth Step on the Journey....

Personal Health

Men's Health has always been one of those things that is seen and not heard. We feel sorry for the Old Boy who has Prostate Cancer, or has been diagnosed with Diabetes, or you're worried about your own Cholesterol getting a little high, but we seem to take little care of ourselves. It's an inbuilt emotion that men don't talk about or get checked for their health as this is seen as weak and men are strong and resilient.

Now I'm not suggesting you all turn into a bunch of whingeing hypochondriacs and see the doctor every time you scratch yourself shaving......but stop being a self-obsessed hero and get a regular 12 month check-up for the key issues. Some simple blood tests and a chat to the Doctor once a year may be the thing that saves your life.

There are a few specific health issues that seem to affect middle aged men more than younger men and whilst this is not meant to be a complete personal health guide, it is an overview of some of the key health issues men should be aware of and once a year just go and get yourself checked.

Cholesterol

Hardening of the arteries with fatty deposits makes blood circulation harder and can create potential heart and stroke conditions. Do yourself a favour and research what foods are problems in this area and as part of your nutritional review make some small changes to the amounts of these foods you consume. A simple blood test will tell you what your cholesterol level is. Acceptable cholesterol levels may differ dependent on an individuals associated health condition but as a general rule you should be under 5.5.

Heart Disease

Often can be hereditary in nature so firstly ask questions about your family history of heart disease. However just because no one in your family has had it before doesn't mean you won't have problems. Talk to your doctor about this and what small measures you can be taking each day to create overall heart health. It goes without saying that smoking is a major issue for heart and all health.

Diabetes

Diabetes is the body's inability to process sugars in the blood. There is a strong link between diabetes and heart disease. It impacts dramatically on your daily life and forces stringent diet control. There are two types of diabetes, Type 2 where the body does not produce enough insulin, and Type 1 where the body produces no insulin. There is little you are able to do to prevent Type 1 diabetes however there is lot you can do to prevent Type 2 diabetes and it all revolves around managing your diet.

Skin Cancer

Of course I'm a Ginger so skin cancer made the list, but just because you have dark skin does not mean you won't get melanoma. In fact people with olive or darker complexions are often more susceptible to melanoma because they did not pay attention to being sun safe. Remember that Bob Marley died of Melanoma that started under the nail on his big toe! So regardless of who you are, get the whole body checked over once a year for skin cancer and weird looking moles.

Prostate Cancer

Prostate Cancer has been the most commonly diagnosed cancer in Australian men in recent times. I have a personal link to this cancer as my father died of prostate cancer at 69. The one thing I always remember him saying, was when the Doctor asked him when did he first notice symptoms, and he realised it had crept up on him so slowly that by the time he even thought there may be a problem it was too late.

The recommendation is to get a full prostate exam every year after you turn 50. By full, I of course mean the digit up the rear track…..and let's face it, who doesn't enjoy that? But I recommend that after 40, part of your annual blood test should be a PSA count. This is a simple blood test that assists in identifying any specific cancer cells in the blood stream and can help with early detection.

TASK:

Of course there are many other health issues you should be aware of so research and get a basic understanding, but the task now is to book an appointment with your Doctor for an overall health check. Then make every year on your birthday the time you go back and get it all checked over again.

Injury Prevention and Management

Warm up and Warm Down

This is probably the most important aspect of longevity in training. Be prepared to take 5 minutes to warm up the joints and muscles with dynamic movements, and 5 minutes to warm down and lengthen the muscles and improve flexibility in the joints and tendons through relaxed static stretching.

Rest Ice Compression Elevation (RICE)

On oldie but a goodie. When you get an injury the first thing you do is stop that exercise and rest the injured area until it is 100% better. Ice the area, 20 minutes on, 20 minutes off for an hour immediately after sustaining the injury. Use a comprehension bandage especially over night when you are asleep. Elevate the injured area as best you can, ideally above your heart so that gravity helps with reducing swelling.

I however add 2 separate elements to this process as follows –

Heat

When the affected area starts to feel a little better, perhaps after a few days, start to utilise a heat rub. What you need to do is start to get blood flowing back into the area so that repair can get underway as quick as possible. Heat will assist with his process, but only after the swelling and bruising has subsided.

Ice Prevention

If you have a particular area of the body that you have injured before and is a weak spot, (knees are a classic example), make sure you ice that vulnerable area after training and heat rub before training every session. This isn't only when you have an injury, this is a permanent action you need to take to assist with longevity. It doesn't matter that you finished training and there is no soreness, if you have a known weak area then ice it after every session and heat it before every session. Prevention is better than cure.

Training under compression

Is it wise to train with a compression bandage? If your injury is severe enough that you can't function without a compression bandage then you should not be working the affected area. Change your exercise routine to avoid stress on that joint or area.

However in the case of an old injury that sometimes flares up I am a believer that wearing a compression bandage assists, but maybe not in the way you think. There is little value in the compression during training and in fact this is restricting blood flow and that can cause problems. There is some advantage in the compression locking the joint into a limited range of motion, but the greatest benefit of training with a compression bandage is that it is a constant reminder of the affected area and will assist you to restrict your movements or adapt your movements around the affected area.

However as soon as you can, get rid of the compression when training and utilise the heat rub warm up and the ice cool down as a more permanent solution.

Adaption Not Excuses

In the end make sure you are honest with yourself. Are you using the injury as an excuse not to train? We're not here to break records so stop using the injury as an excuse and adapt your routine to suit.

As the great Philosopher Sgt 'Gunny' Highway once said……
Improvise, Adapt, Overcome.

SOUL

Hippie Jim from Muddy Bay

A feeble ray of light falls briefly on my back,
from fast decaying sunlight,
through the curtains tiny crack,

of an office space in Richmond Tower,
a dingy little space,
Bailiffs court no. 2, the job I love to hate.

Serve a notice, deliver a summons, lives of petty crime.
Then on the train with thugs and grubs,
who wouldn't know the time,

of day I rose this morning with coffee and a smoke.
Life in the city, life as a bailiff,
what a flamin' joke.

But today a file caught my eye as it passed by in tray way.
A summons to be delivered,
to a place called Muddy Bay.

Somewhere in the rainforests of far north Queensland cape.
Where a bloke called simply 'Hippie Jim',
had obviously tried to escape.

Now Hippie Jim was an interesting man, a top flight lawyer they say.
Embezzled his partners and broke the firm,
then escaped to Muddy Bay.

So I booked a plane, a car and a boat, for t'was a difficult place to reach,

Soul

and off I went a bailiff's clerk,
to deliver justice on the beach.

I flew, I drove, I sailed, then eventually I came,
to a beautiful palm fringed beach,
that did not justify its name.

And past the palms in the rainforest trees sat a tiny brown thatched dwelling.
And beside the hut a hammock swayed,
in time with the ocean swelling.

I struggled up the sand, my trousers wet, my shoes had taken a swim,
and was met by a beard, sarong, and bong…..
This must be 'Hippie Jim'.
I opened my mouth to greet the man I intended to take down,

but before I could he smiled and said,
"A VB or a Crown?"
It was late and I was tired, my face was all a frown,
But the more I thought the less I cared….
"I think I'll have a Crown".

And so I sat and watched the sun disappear over Muddy Bay.
Sharing a beer with the criminal,
I was sent to put away.

"You know why I'm here" I said to Jim, "Of course" was his reply,
"You're just doing your job,
but let me tell you so was I."

"I worked for years in the world of law, Stanton, Bryce and Dow.
Really we should have changed our name,
to 'Do we Cheat 'em and How"

"Insurance fraud, accident claims, whatever, we didn't care.
When old mother Hubbard went to the cupboard,
you could be sure we'd stripped it bare."

"We overcharged, we under delivered, we grew rich and we grew fat,
on the misfortunes of our clients,
and we didn't give a rats."

"Then over the years I began to wonder, what the point of all this was,
and the more I thought, the less I liked,
the person who was the cause."

"Of all the greed and all the deceit, and so I made a pact.
I decided to redeem myself,
and hence committed the act."

"Quietly and deceitfully, I laundered all the fees.
Through bank accounts and special bonds,
all located overseas."

"And all the while my business partners didn't even suspect.
Content that ripping the poor man off,
was done with the utmost respect."

Soul

"And now you find me here on the beach, alone and quite content.
But I bet you're wondering, if he's got so much money, why does he live in a tent?"

"Well there isn't any money, that's the best part you see,
I gave it all back to the people,
who need it more than me."

"Redemption son is what I was seeking, not more wealth and fame.
Call me Robin Hood if you like,
but I couldn't live with the shame."

"And so feel free to take me in, I've made peace with him,
But stay the night, we'll have a few beers,
and then you can arrest Jim."

**

A feeble ray of sunlight falls briefly on my back,
from fast decaying sunlight,
through the curtains tiny crack.

And I stop and think of Hippie Jim, and wonder where he is,
And that summons I delivered,
To the bottom of the sea.

JR

Soul
The First Step on the Journey....

What is Soul?

First and foremost....it's not Religion.

The word Soul is used by some religions to describe your life force, or that part of God in you. But Soul is also used to describe a type of music that engenders a feeling of connection and can take you away from the present moment.

These various different uses for the word Soul are not actually that dissimilar and they both try to explain something that is intangible but has deep feeling and meaning for us as individuals. As I said in the introduction, my definition is as follows –

Soul is intangible. It is the meaning for existence. The reason we get up in the morning, and the reason we want to keep pushing forward when things aren't so good.

Soul encompasses so many different parts of our nature, and has such personal significance once you open your mind and thinking to the notion, that it deserves to stand as one of the 4 Pillars of life.

Soul is an intensely personal Journey and as such is not something easily shared with others. Unlike the journey through Body and a lot of the Journey through Mind, where sharing your thinking and goals with others can be motivating and liberating, I believe that your Journey through Soul is something

> *Have an open mind. There is no black and white, only shades of grey.*
>
> ***JR***

you would only share with someone who you have an incredibly close bond. It is such an intangible concept and is one of those things that you know what you mean deep inside but you find it very difficult to articulate into words. It is of course up to what is best for you, but I know from my own personal experience my Journey through Soul has not been something I have shared with others.

But you're writing a book and telling the world, is what I hear you say. I have been on my Journey now for 47 years and it has never been something I have discussed with others, not even my wife. Even writing this book I am sitting in my lounge on a Saturday afternoon with the cricket in the background (Australia is 6/50 by the way!!) and it still feels intensely personal, but I feel I have reached a destination on my continuing journey, where I feel I have an obligation to share my thoughts with others. But believe me, this has taken a long time and a lot of personal growth to get to this spot.

This Journey through Soul will ask you first and foremost to be open to concepts that to some of you, may seem New Age or only for the realm of Hippies and Greenies. That negative attitude or Automatic Thought, is one of the key locked doors that are standing in front of you and stopping you from living a life worth living. It is an attitude that is closed to anything different, and why is that? When you boil it down it comes back to our basic survival instincts –

If something is different and I or my 'tribe' don't understand it, it may be a threat and hence we attack it to neutralise the threat.

Or looking at another angle, if I do something that is not understood by my tribe they may turn against me.

It's all about your basic instinct of survival, what will others think? It's got nothing to do with you genuinely thinking it is stupid and has no place in the world, that is only the defence mechanism.

Now I'm not asking all *Old Boys* to go out and join a cult, shave your head, and start chanting incantations, but what I am asking, (and this is fundamental to changing our attitudes and to taking back control of your life and living a life worth living), is to have an open mind. Look and learn without judgement. Not every way of life is for every person, but at least recognise that your way of life is not for everyone. Understand there are many great and happy people who have very different attitudes and lifestyles to what you have now. Take a step outside your circle of influence, broaden your understanding of the world and how other people live their lives.

TASK:

Think about your attitude to people who think differently. Are you set in your ways and everything is Black and White? Remember there is no Black and White, only shades of grey. Can you open your mind and look at other ways of living, without immediately judging them? This is such a fundamental element of changing your life for the better. It doesn't mean you immediately have to accept anything that comes your way, it just asks that you take a cautious little step out of the dark and into the grey areas…….

Soul
The Second Step on the Journey....

The Subconscious Master

Our conscious mind, the voice in our head, what occupies our thoughts at each moment, reflects only a small portion of what is going on upstairs. There are countless scientific studies and reports into the balance between our Conscious and Subconscious minds, and on average most generally point towards our conscious mind being only 10% of the activity in our top paddock. 90% of our emotions, actions and reactions, are borne from our subconscious mind.

How is our Subconscious Formed?

Over our lifetime of experience we take in all our experiences through the 5 senses, Visual (See), Auditory (Hear), Kinaesthetic (Feel), Gustatory (Taste), and Olfactory (Smell). We then filter those experiences in our brains based on our values. Our values are established through both Nature (hereditary traits), and Nurture (How we're brought up and what we experience). From this filtering we start to establish Core Beliefs, which are ways in which we view the world, and every subsequent experience is viewed through the filters of our Core Belief, which provides an Automatic Thought about an experience, which creates a certain behaviour towards the experience, which then reinforces the Core Belief.

> *"Everything we hear is an opinion, everything we see is a perspective, not the truth."*
>
> **Marcus Aurelius, Roman Emperor and Philosopher**

This is how stereotypes, and small minded thinking can get a grip in your life. The problem is that Core Beliefs become part of our subconscious and we won't even question them or our Automatic Thoughts, we accept them as truth. Of course in our view of the world they are real.

Our View of the World is Relative

This is such an important concept to understand. Two people can have a very different view of a situation depending on their core beliefs and automatic thoughts. The saying 'Perception is Reality' is so very true.

Here's a simple example –

You're in a meeting with an employee discussing the current project and its status. Your employee starts to get agitated about your questioning why the project is behind time. They get angry when you suggest they can do better they then shut down and won't engage in conversation anymore. You get agitated yourself as this is typical of employees these days, they just don't work hard enough and won't even try.

The employee though has come into this meeting knowing the project is behind. They have been working hard but he is currently going through a messy divorce, and he hasn't seen his kids in two weeks. He can't afford to lose this job but does not want to bring his personal life into the matter as an excuse. He gets angry because he can't provide an adequate reason to his boss for the project being behind and decides it's better to say nothing than fall apart in front of his boss.

Now it's easy to say, if you're the boss, "Well if I'd known the facts I would have reacted differently, so therefore it was because I didn't have the required knowledge of the situation".

No that is incorrect. You as the boss had an automatic thought and assumed without second thought, that the employee was just lazy, and when they didn't engage with you it was just evidence of their guilt. There was no room in your thoughts for an alternate reality.

That was a situation of fact, where the facts of the issues being faced by the employee were the real reason for the problems, and communication was missing from the process. But what about a different environment such as the Victim Mentality? This is where a person's perception of reality is so afflicted by past negative experience that the facts of a situation can be distorted no matter how obvious. Let's use the same example above but in a different context –

The boss calls his employee into a meeting to discuss the project and why it is behind time. The boss wants to get to the bottom of the issue and find out what is holding things up. The boss is considered in his questions and is looking for the real reasons so he can provide solutions and get everyone on the same page.

You as the employee get the message from your boss to come in and discuss the project. Your immediate reaction is one of disdain for the boss. He's always onto me about this project. I'm doing the best I can. I have all these problems and he can't even see it. Why do these bad things always happen to me? I'll probably lose this job now and it's all because of my ex-wife. The boss questions me about the project and do I need extra resources to get it back on track. So he's suggesting I am not good enough to finish this report on my own, of course that's what he thinks. He just wants to get rid of me I know it.

Perception is Reality

JR

This all sounds melodramatic but it happens every day in every workplace in the world. Each party to an experience brings their own perception of not only what the problem is all about, but also what the solution is, or who to blame. We spend so much time wrapped up in justifying our own perceptions that we don't open our minds to the potential that there may be another reality.

And why do we do this? Again it's the survival instinct. Your perception of a situation comes about because you apply everything you believe to be true about your view of the world, and if your view of the world happens to be wrong then that may constitute a threat to who you are as a person, and hence we spend time and energy reinforcing our own view of the world because its makes us feel safe and in control.

We debate, argue and defend our position and view of the world. Having an opinion is not wrong, but defending that opinion or filtered view of the world, without any thought to an alternate scenario, only causes conflict. Having the confidence in yourself to be able to accept that another person's version of reality, is as real to them as your view and opinion is to you, is an amazingly liberating feeling.

How the Subconscious works on a World Scale

The subconscious is not just an individual thing but is also a collective. Core Beliefs and Automatic Thoughts can be part of a group of people, a religious group, a race of people, or a nation of people. This is how wars start, when a collective belief becomes an automatic belief and the collective rallies together to fight those who are different to our group beliefs.

Social Media is an excellent example of people's subconscious automatic thoughts being expressed. Social Media communication lacks the temperance of face to face communication and hence the intent of messages can get lost without the addition of body language and physical contact for a message. Without these additional communication tools, much is left up to peoples interpretation of the message, and that interpretation is based on the receiver's individual perception of the world.

On Social Media people feel they can judge others with little responsibility for the impact their judgements or words have. I hear people say that Social Media allows people to express their true selves, but it doesn't. What it does is allow people to express their subconscious and distorted views of the world. Social Media seems to have led to more intolerance and judgement, than open communication.

How do we overcome this?

Be aware of your automatic thoughts about any experience you have. Remember to listen to the voice in your head, it is the gateway to your automatic thoughts. Understand that your subconscious will make an immediate and automatic judgement of a situation based on your past collective life experiences and your core beliefs.

When you become aware you are doing this, this is the first step towards gaining control of your attitudes and emotions. It is unlocking a door that has been barred to you, and is barred to most people most of their lives, and they just can't see it.

When you become aware you are having an automatic thought or are judging a situation, stop and investigate what other alternative stories could there be that would also make this story real. If someone is late for work and you immediately think 'they are always late', what other story could have led to this person being late for work?

TASK:

Think of a situation or person that brings stress into your life. Write down what your immediate and automatic thoughts are about this person or situation. Why do they bring stress into your life or make you feel that way? What is the story you believe is true about this person or situation?

Now try looking at this situation as if you are a third person. Get imaginative and come up with alternative stories as to why this person is the way they are, or why this situation stresses you. Try to think completely opposite to your current belief. Tell the story as if you were that person or the situation. How would you justify being that way or come up with a reason that justifies the situation as it is.

This is a very hard exercise and will be a test as to how well you can separate you as a person from your circumstances. It will reflect how aware you are of your subconscious automatic beliefs. If you just can't come up with an alternate scenario for that person or situation then your subconscious is in control of you. You don't have to believe the alternate stories you come up with to justify the person or the situation that stresses you, it's about getting you to understand that there are two sides to every story. Regardless of how much you believe your version of realty, the other person totally believes their version. To understand this is a great step forward in understanding others and reducing stress in your own life.

Soul
The Third Step on the Journey....

The Energy Circle

As we've discussed your personal reality is real to you, just as real as the next persons reality is to them. Both of you could be having the same experience but having a completely different view of the reality of what is happening. This is due to your Core Beliefs that have been built up over a lifetime of experiences, and become your subconscious automatic thoughts and your perception of reality.

One of the major problems with the world has always been that people will defend their perception of reality with their lives if necessary, rather than open their minds to a possible different version of reality that could be just as legitimate as the view they hold.

Part of the interaction we have with all people is our energy fields. If you think this is just new-age hippie crap, then get out and read some scientific literature. All matter has a gravitational field, not just planets and stars, but even humans and all forms of matter regardless of how small. In humans that energy field is affected dramatically by the people around us and the information we receive on a daily basis. We all know that person who can suck the colour out of a rainbow just by entering a room, and that person who is just fun to be around. This is the energy that person projects, and the impact on you is how you perceive reality and how that energy affects your emotions, mood and attitude. It is a very powerful force and is the basis of a whole line of psychological and scientific study, but be assured it is very real. We tend not to notice because we just assume that negative person is a pain in the arse and it's their fault you are now in a bad mood. It's not their fault, it's your fault, you have allowed the energy they projected to be taken in by your subconscious and it then reveals itself in your changed state of being.

Energy fields between humans are infectious. The 'Mob Mentality' is the classic example. One person in a group starts a fight and next minute everyone is in on the act. Soccer hooligans are a classic example. Look at the energy at a music concert. When any concert starts it's generally a bit subdued but then a couple of people stand up and start dancing and by the end of the night the room is rocking and everyone is up and having a great time (a few beers also helps).

I have developed what I call the ***Energy Field Model of Personal Reality (EFM)*** to try and explain how the energy fields of situations and other people affects and impacts your own view of the world and creates your own personal reality.

The EMF is a self-perpetuating circle of shared energy that creates our version of reality, and works something like the following –

We are surrounded by people, situations, events, social media, news and a multitude of other things (let's call them 'Stuff') that impact on us. In these modern times the internet has made us so connected to the whole world that something that is happening in the USA and Iraq that is shown on the news or social media, can impact us significantly, yet 50 years ago we were much less impacted by events outside our sphere of influence. The problem is our sphere of influence now takes in the whole world.

The Energy Circle

All this 'Stuff' is both positive and negative. Some 'Stuff' makes us happy and some make us sad. Other 'Stuff' make us confident and other 'Stuff' creates anxiety. We take all this 'Stuff' in through our 5 senses (Seeing, hearing, feeling, tasting, smelling), and we process it with conscious thought, which is the voice in our head. We use our own internal language to describe to ourselves what we are sensing. You know when you see a situation you don't like your internal dialogue will make statements about what you think at that time, or if you are faced with a dangerous situation your internal dialogue will feel the sense of panic.

All this information we take in is processed and filtered through our Core Beliefs. Remember our Core Beliefs are those things that we believe subconsciously to be true. They have been built up over a lifetime of experiences and we don't question their validity. This filtered information is then saved in our Subconscious, just like on the hard drive of a computer, and reaffirms existing Core Beliefs, or creates new Core Beliefs.

Our subconscious is then the auto-pilot of our lives. When we are faced with 'Stuff' our subconscious tells us what to think or how to behave, by producing Automatic Thoughts, Actions and Reactions.

These Automatic Thoughts, Actions and Reactions are then pushed out into the world as our own energy, and this creates our own Personal Reality. It dictates how the 'Stuff' responds to us and interact with us……..and so the cycle continues.

Not only does the Energy of other external 'Stuff' impact on us, but so does the way we act and behave impact on our own Energy and either reinforces or questions our own personal reality.

This is how people become so stuck in a negative state. They perceive a majority of negative energy from all the external 'Stuff' they surround themselves with, this in turn impacts how they see the world, and creates automatic thoughts about the world around them, which is broadcast out to the world via their negative Thoughts, Actions and Reactions, which ensures that they continually see negative 'Stuff' around them because this is their Personal Reality.

The Energy Circle

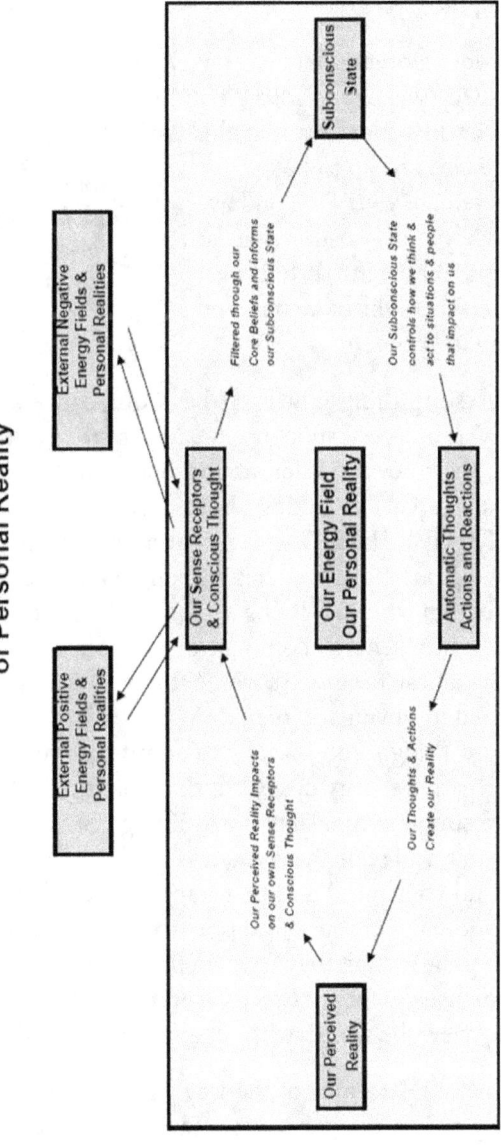

Breaking the Cycle

So how do we break this cycle? Well how hard it is depends on how deeply subconsciously you live your life. How much are you set in your ways that this is the way things are and everyone else can go to hell? How opinionated are you? Do you have strong views on various issues? Are you a Black and White person, it's either right or wrong and there's no in between?

> *Sometimes you don't know you're trapped until you've been freed.*
>
> *JR*

The interesting thing is when I have this conversation with people who are very subconsciously entrenched, they argue with me that they are tolerant and open thinkers and that I don't know what I'm talking about…………………..THERE IT IS RIGHT THERE! The fact that a person gets defensive about being questioned, or has a strong opinion that they are right and I am wrong, is living a subconscious life. They are at the mercy of the energy coming from the 'Stuff' around them and they just can't see it. It's ironic that you can't see that you are trapped until you are free.

It is a hard thing to do initially to admit that you are caught in this negative energy cycle, but that's ok, small steps. There are some simple initial steps I call Energy Breakers, that you can take that will really help you take some big strides towards opening up your mind and being able to see the trap you are in. I've put many of these into practice with my clients and it is amazing the impact they have on their lives. It enables them to 'see' themselves for the first time and look at themselves and how they view the world, without any personal judgement.

Being able to take a look at the way you are can only be done effectively if you can do it without judging yourself. If you look at the way you did something and you immediately call yourself a loser, or you are embarrassed at how you handled the situation, or you are embarrassed at what others thought, then you are still entrenched in subconscious living. Having an open and non-judgemental mind does not mean it only applies to the external 'Stuff'. Of **NUMBER 1 IMPORTANCE** is the ability to look at yourself without judgement. If you can't be kind to yourself then you will never be kind to others.

Looking at yourself without judgement does not mean you lower your standards. It does not mean you look at the way you are lazy and say well that's ok I am not judging myself. That is apathy and laziness in itself and means that you are not clear on your values and how you want to live your life. What you must do is be able to look at the fact you are lazy, see and feel the reasons why you can't motivate yourself, accept that your lack of motivation is something that is impacting on you, and then look for some ways to improve on that, slowly with baby steps.

So some of those initial simple steps you can take towards changing your Energy Circle and your Personal Reality are –

- **Surround yourself with more positive people.**

Take an inventory of who you are surrounded with every day. Who impacts on you positively and who impacts on you negatively. Try to spend a little less time with the negative people and seek out more time with the positive people

- **Stop Watching the News**

This is a great little tool to try for a few weeks. Do not listen to or read any news. No nightly news, no newspapers, no TV news. 'But I need to know what's going on in the world, it's important I stay up to date!' WHY? The world will go on without you. Nothing will change if you stop listening for a while. You will not fall apart or be unprepared if some tragic event happens. What makes you think you would be any more prepared because you had kept up to date with the world and then something happened?

We all know the news is terribly negative. You can't turn on the TV or read a paper without seeing or hearing of another terrorist attack, the war in the middle east, local crime gangs, kids breaking into houses etc. etc. etc.

This is incredible negative energy that we take in every day. How do you think this impacts our Energy Field and our view of the World and hence our Personal Reality?

It's not irresponsible to stop taking in this negative news….I would argue it is the only way you will grow as a person and become a more positive and better person. Another more positive person in the world has to be better than one more negative one.

- **Be Less Connected**

Our modern world has us so connected. Email, mobile phones, Facebook, YouTube, Instagram, Twitter, etc. etc. We are always taking in 'Stuff', there is simply no downtime anymore. As Old Boys you'll remember when you were kids and there were no mobile phones or email or internet, or at least you weren't allowed to have access to them every second of the day. We played in the backyard after school. We spent time with friends actually talking and playing. We disconnected from school and we were able to change our thought patterns for a while. Now we check Facebook before we go to bed and as soon as we get up in the morning. We have work emails at 10pm at night and 5am in the morning. We take work calls on the weekends and holidays.

Now it's a fact of life that the world is connected and will only become more so, but that is no excuse not to plan downtime, and planning is what we have to do. Downtime in today's society doesn't just happen, it must be planned. Take time to be alone with no phone, email or other. It sounds easy but this is a very hard thing to do. It's the survival instinct in play again, especially when it comes to work. If I don't stay on top of things I'll lose my job. Of course if you just let stuff slide and never deal with it then you probably will lose your job, but that is not what we are talking about here. It's about managing your life and your connections with the world.

For example some changes I have made in my own life that have been an enormous benefit are as follows –

- **I stopped receiving emails on my mobile**

I now only get my emails to my Laptop. At first I was dubious and thought I need to be on top of this, but I realised that what was happening was that I was double handling. I would see the email on my mobile, read it, be unable to respond until I got back to the office, worry about it until then, then read it again when I got back to the office. This not only saved me time but reduced my stress levels

- **I turn my mobile off and compartmentalise phone calls**

I do not take every phone call as soon as it comes in, I often turn off my phone and let them go to message bank. But I have a rule that I will always return every call before the day is out. I found when I was working hard on a project, the mobile phone interruptions not only stop my work but they stop my train of thought and for each 5 minute phone call I was losing 10 minutes by the time I got my head back in the game.

I make all my phone calls when I am finished the task at hand and I can clear my head, or in my car between meetings when I am free to talk. There will be a lot more on this in our Time Management section.

- **I deleted Facebook off my mobile**

I got into a bad habit of checking Facebook whenever I had a spare minute, before bed, when I woke up, and on the toilet (come on you know you do…)

I kept my Facebook account as I still wanted to be connected but I deleted it off my phone so it was not as easy to quickly open it up and scroll through for 10 minutes every hour.

TASK:

Understand that other people see the world very differently to you, they have their own Personal Realities, and that their truth is as real to them as yours is to you. It doesn't make them right or wrong, it doesn't make you right or wrong. What makes it wrong is if we defend our position with no regard to the 'other side of the coin'.

Think about something you have an opinion about. Now think about the person who would have the exact opposite opinion. Now sit down and right some dot points as if you were that other person and you are justifying your opinion. It's very hard to separate from your reality and see it from another reality, so start with something that you have an opinion on but if you had to you could see some points of view of the other person. Remember small steps, don't rush straight into your opinion on Religion……..bit of a big one to start with. The aim is to simply become aware that there is always two sides to every story…....always….it doesn't make them right or wrong, it just makes it so.

Second task is to try the Energy Breakers listed as detailed above. Try and do them for 5 days, Monday to Friday. See what impact each one has. 5 days isn't enough to get you past the feeling that being disconnected is a bad thing, but it's a start. Once you have completed 5 days have a break for a few days and then try a 2 week stint. Don't try them all at once, just do one at a time, ease into it.

- Surround yourself with more positive people.
- Stop Watching the News
- Be Less Connected

Soul
The Fourth Step on the Journey....

Loathing Life....or....Living Life

This book is all about being an *Old Boy*. But be very clear on the distinction between being and *Old Boy* and being an **Old Man**.

An **Old Man** is not an age based thing, it is an attitude. Being locked into your opinions of the world, being quick to defend your position, being quick to point out why others are wrong, and scoffing at those who try and are different, are all elements of being an Old Man. You close yourself off from alternate ideas, and you close yourself off from life.

There are many aspects to the life of a middle aged man but everyone is different and different circumstances affect people in different ways. But what remains static is how, at this stage of life, middle aged men start to view the world.

It's at this age that attitude can take two distinct paths –

Loathing Life (Old Man)

Especially in middle age, we begin to question and wonder at life's purpose. We try to understand why we are where we are. The dreams we had as young men have not worked out as planned, we measure our lot in life and it doesn't seem to be much. With this thinking our attitudes start to harden. Things become very black and white, with our opinions becoming hard and fast about what is right and what is wrong. We start to look for reasons that we have not achieved as we think we should have. We look for people or situations to blame. We live in the past and blame others (the government, the immigrants, the Muslims, the stupid neighbour next door) for all life's troubles, and we ignore the future for fear of continued perceived failure.

Living Life *(Old Boy)*

But there is another avenue that a few men take. They also question life and the way the world works, and they acknowledge that the world is unfair and that suffering seems to be the normal state of play. But the difference is they start to realise that happiness is personal. It is an attitude and a state of mind. They accept that they have influence but not control over external circumstances and happenings in the world, and that if they think things around them need to work out for the best for them to be happy, then they are doomed to loathing life.... and that is not how they want to feel and live for the rest of their lives.

So they start the search for meaning and decide to make a difference in their own world, with the things they can control, with the people they love, and live life to the fullest in the best way they can.

Both **Loathing** and **Living** life are self-fulfilling attitudes. The more you travel down one path the more entrenched you become in that way of living. This is a classic example of the Energy Circle and the Energy Field Model. The energy you surround yourself with creates your subconscious, which manifests itself in your attitude, actions and reactions. This then gives off its own energy and attracts the same type of people and situations (energy) into your life, and reinforces your attitude, and the cycle continues and strengthens itself in the process.

But how can you change from Loathing Life to Living Life?

Remember the Energy Field Model is a cyclical process, it is not linear, and there is no start or end point. What that means is that you can break into this cycle at any point in the process. What is amazing is how vulnerable the Energy Field is to change. The smallest changes that enter the cyclical process cannot do anything other than flow through the whole system. The reason we think it is hard to change is because we are so entrenched in our own subconscious attitudes. We believe so strongly that our view of reality is right that any attempt to challenge that reality, or challenge any area of the Energy Field, is generally met with resistance from our subconscious. But if you are able to just open the door to the possibility of something different, a different view of what your life could be, then the energy model starts to change immediately.

> *Do you Loathe life, or do you Live life?*

I'm not talking about radical change and flinging that door wide open, that isn't something your subconscious will accept and it will fight back hard. I am talking about a very subtle, under the radar, easy to achieve, level of change. In the Third Step on The Journey I spoke about some simple concrete tasks you can do to affect your Energy Field which are also helpful in this process, but to change from Loathing to Living life is a more holistic approach and requires some self-investigation and acceptance that maybe some of your opinions and attitudes are not 100% correct 100% of the time.

This isn't a simple attitude to crack, but you will be amazed how when the smallest initial crack appears in your Energy Field, it's like the flood gates opening. I have found one of the simplest and easiest ways to give your Energy Field a nudge is to **Stop Voicing Your Opinion**. Every time you realise you are starting to voice an opinion on a person, a situation, or you find you are defending a view of the world that you have, just **STOP**. You are not being weak or 'not standing up for your principles', you are simply keeping your opinion to yourself and listening and watching. You aren't agreeing with other people's views of the world, you are simply observing what is going on around you.

Its hard work constantly having an opinion and defending your view of the world and it is such a refreshing and fulfilling feeling to stop. It takes a while for you to become conscious of when you are being opinionated or defending your reality. At first you will have had an opinion or even been in an argument and an hour or so later when you have calmed down you will realise what you were doing, but if you keep practicing it will slowly come to mind earlier until you are able to just observe without having to voice your opinion or feeling the need to defend your view.

This is such a powerful tool to be able to master. If you are strongly entrenched in your personal reality and opinions, initially this approach may leave you feeling angry because you didn't 'stand up for yourself', but remember what you are defending? You are defending your view of who you are as a person, not your physical wellbeing. It is not a life and death issue, but it's real to your subconscious because your subconscious is only made up of your thoughts and opinions.

Please persevere and keep practicing because what starts to happen is you grow in self-confidence. You don't feel the need to have to defend your opinion, you feel confident that you can observe others without feeling threatened. This not only provides you with a new found sense of who you are, but because you no longer feel the need to defend your opinions or views, you now have the confidence to question some of your views and opinions, and then you are really starting to Live Life.

TASK:

Think about a recent situation where you had an opinion on an issue.

- What was the issue?
- What was your opinion?
- Why did you feel you had to voice your opinion?
- What opposite opinions on this issue do other people have?
- Visualise how the scene would have played out if you simply didn't voice your opinion?

Moving forward I want you to become aware every time you have an opinion, or every time you feel the need to defend your view of something. Then every time you become aware I want you to write down what the issue was that you had an opinion on or were defending, and ask yourself the above questions.

Slowly as you start to become more aware you will start to recognise situations where you are about to voice an opinion or defend a position. Just take the time to stop and listen. Keep your view to yourself no matter how much you want to defend it, and then afterwards I want you to write down the situation, your view, the other persons view, and how you felt when you kept your views to yourself.

There are 4 distinct stages of personal development with this approach as follows -

1. Initially you will be aware that you are voicing your opinion but you don't stop as you need to defend yourself

2. In the next stage you will be able to keep your views to yourself but you will feel a sense of frustration that you should have defended your position or stood up for yourself

3. At stage 3 you will be able to keep your views to yourself and listen to others opinions and views. This is an enlightening stage where you start to see how much other people are entrenched in their own personal realities. Because of this you are able to listen more with empathy than anything else, as to how unconscious these people are of their limited personal reality.

4. And finally with this awareness of how other people are stuck in their subconscious you will be able to respond to others views from the point of view of understanding that their opinions are coming from a very subconscious place and that it does not affect your self-confidence. It's at this stage you will be able to discuss different points of view without feeling threatened.

Soul
The Fifth Step on the Journey....

A Life's Purpose.....Don't worry if you don't have one

As humans we are in a constant search for some meaning to our lives, whether we are aware of it or not. Some people pronounce they are just a 'go with the flow' kind of guy, but in their quiet moments they too wonder what it's all about. Why do others achieve and I haven't? How did I get to where I am in life? Why do I worry about things? I want to achieve this or that because then I will be happy.

These are all different ways in which we seek a purpose in life. We recognise most of them as everyday worries and concerns, but the reason we have concerns and desires is because we want to make something of ourselves, we don't want to just 'Exist'.

The problem comes however that when we start to drill down into what your life's purpose is, many people start to get frustrated, angry, or even just close off to the discussion. This is because we are conditioned through the media and society in general, that we should have a strong understanding of who we are and what we are striving for in our lives, and when we realise we have no idea what we really want or where we are going, we get depressed or anxious and we feel like we have failed ourselves.

Straight up and right now..... Give up worrying about it. Stop thinking you MUST have a purpose in life, or that if you don't have any meaning in your life then you are a failure. We are conditioned by society to think we must have direction, but News Flash......NO ONE has every aspect of their life fulfilled with meaning and direction all of the time.

This is important to understand……...No one has **EVERY ASPECT** of their lives fulfilled with meaning and direction **ALL OF THE TIME**.

Firstly, Meaning in Life is not one thing, it is many different things for many different parts of our lives, and at times we may feel like we have meaning in one area of our lives but that every other area is out of control. Sometimes work is going well and we value what we are doing, but our family life is in turmoil. Other times we feel a strong desire to get ourselves physically fit and work hard towards it and feel a real sense of purpose, but our friendships have taken a back seat and we feel something has been lost.

> *A Life's Purpose is a misleading statement. It should read Life's Purposes. Multiple areas of your life require multiple purposes. One size does not fit all.*
>
> *JR*

Secondly, meaning, goals, and purpose, change all the time. As you grow older, as you change jobs, as you grow a family, and as simple as your mood changes, then so too does our meaning of life change. Our purpose for 'being' is forever changing and if we think we can't change with it then we are doomed to a life of inaction, frustration and depression.

What I am trying to get across to you is that the Media and Society portray that an individual who is strong and in control has a focused and singular purpose, and they chase that purpose with relentless vigour. That is such bullshit and could not be further from real life, but unfortunately our subconscious is conditioned to think that is what society expects, and if I am not like that then I am an underachiever.

A Life's Purpose is not one single thing.

It's important to realise that to have a purpose or meaning in your life, is many things to an individual. Family, career, work, compassionate giving back, health and wellness, spiritual growth, and any other thing you can think of that is important to you. And every individual is different, so what has meaning to you may have no meaning to the next person.

It is an intensely private thing, having purpose in life.

If you stop focusing on a single element to bring meaning to your life, and understand that you may have a dozen different meanings or purposes in your life that cover the various different areas of your life, you will start to open up your thinking and stop feeling a sense of failure, by realising that just because one area of your life doesn't seem to be working out, there are many other areas that you can create some meaning and purpose in. Don't put all your eggs in one basket.

A Life's Purpose is in a constant state of change.

Then just when you think you've found purpose or meaning for a part of your life, all of a sudden it doesn't feel quite right. It's at this point that we think we just don't get it and you have no idea what's going on, and we tend to give up and decide to live subconsciously, with our automatic thoughts driving our emotions, actions, and reaction, to all of life's experiences.

Be clear in your understanding, that a purpose or meaning is not necessarily a long term thing. Through your life you may have a multitude of purposes or meanings for different areas of your life, which change as you grow older and wiser, and experience more of life's ups and downs. It is highly unusual to have a singular purpose in an area of your life that remains unchanged over a lifetime, and I would go as far as to say, that if someone does have that then they are closed off from change and perhaps can't see all that life has to offer.

Of course there are people like Mother Theresa who have dedicated their lives to a cause, but remember what we see and experience as the Mother Theresa phenomena is what the media portrays to us. Have you met Mother Theresa? Do you know how she thought on a day to day basis? Do you know how her purpose in life changed over time? Again this comes back to the media and society portraying a singularly focused human……I bet she was much more complex than that.

The point is, be accepting of change. Accept that as you grow older, as you experience more of life, and as you grow as a person, that your idea of your Life's Purpose or what gives your life meaning, will change. Go with it, don't try and swim against the stream…..its hard work and you end up nowhere.

What if you have no purpose in any area of your life all the time?

As we have discussed, you will likely never have purpose and meaning in every area of your life at one time. When something is going well for you, there is generally another area of your life that has taken a back seat or is giving you trouble. There will even be times when you think nothing is going well in your life and your life has no purpose. These can be dark troubling times and it's at these times we really need someone else to be able to talk to, someone who can look at your life without judgement. It's at these times that we can't see the forest for the trees so to speak, and by opening up to a friend who we respect and know will not judge us, we give ourselves an opportunity to find that purpose and meaning that is currently hiding from us.

Talking to someone does not mean seeing a therapist or life coach, although these are great tools if you want to use them. In its simplest form, and the best format for an *Old Boy*, is just have a beer with a mate and just talk. Many *Old Boys* won't do this for fear of looking weak or not 'manly' enough, but you will be amazed at how much a mate will want to help you.

Another avenue to getting yourself out of a slump and discovering some purpose for yourself, is to help someone else out. Be the mate who has a beer and talks with his friend about their problems.

When I was at boarding school back in the early 1980's there was a Christian Brother who had an enormous influence on my life, Brother Mark (Ruggy) Murphy. I didn't understand it at the time, but years later I realised some of the things he said and how he conducted himself, became guides for myself and my actions. One of the things he said to me once when I was about 13, that is relevant to this discussion, is that if you have a problem the best way to resolve it is to help someone else with their problem. I've tried this many times over the years and it is an incredible way to be able to look at your own problems without judgement by seeing yourself through the problems of the person you are helping. So never hesitate to be the mate who takes a troubled friend for a beer and a chat, it helps you as well not just him.

The Energy Field Model and a Life's Purpose

Searching for a Life's Purpose is an energy field on its own, and by utilising the **Energy Field Model**, we can see how our outcomes are impacted.

Firstly from an outward perspective, the energy we receive from people we surround ourselves with and situations we engage with, impacts on our own energy field and impacts what we think about regularly, how we think about the things that happen to us, and why we think we are the way we are. These all impact on every part of our life and can lead to good or bad energy, and hence good or bad outcomes in terms of what we think our Life's Purpose is. Be conscious of who you surround yourself with, and what experiences you allow yourself to be a part of.

Secondly there is a strong internal **Energy Field Model** that has a significant impact on our outcomes. As we discussed having a Life's Purpose is not a singular thing, nor does it relate to a singular part of your life. You will have different purposes and meanings for different parts of your life at different times. This means that sometimes a part of your life such as physical health may be going just the way you want to, but your family life is in disarray.

So think of each part of your life as a separate energy field on its own –

- Family
- Career
- Financial

- Physical
- Social
- Spiritual
- Etc.

From your physical life you may have purpose and meaning at this time which is projecting positive energy into your own energy field, but problems at home and with family are projecting a negative energy field. Which one wins the battle? Remember the old saying –

Q. There are two beasts inside you, one is good and one is bad, and they are at war. Which one wins the battle?

A. The one you feed.

Try to avoid giving too much energy (thought and reaction) to the negative areas of your life.

Compartmentalise your life. Don't look at your life as one singular beast that can't be tamed. Break it down into the various different areas of your life and accept that sometimes some areas are going ok and other areas are completely up the creek. But be thankful for the positive areas, no matter how small. As humans we always understate the positives and overstate the negatives, because that is a survival mechanism. So be aware of this, be aware that your subconscious is doing this to you, and stop stressing about having to have it all together.

I've always thought in my life I was the full six-pack…..I just didn't have the little plastic bit that holds them all together, and that's ok, they're easier to drink that way.

A Life's Purpose.....Don't worry if you don't have one

TASK:

Think about, and write down, all the areas of your life that are important to you right now.

In each area then list all the things that you would like to be better about that part of your life.

Write down how you feel about those areas that could be improved and think about why you may be stuck in that position. Is it the people you surround yourself with? Is it the situations you find yourself in? Then above all remember it isn't the people or the situation itself, but it's how you interpret the experience of that person or that situation. So ask yourself why you react the way you do to that person or that situation

Once you've completed that exercise, go through every area of your life again and list the positives, no matter how small. This can be difficult as we will downplay the positives, but simply having a house to live in and food for your next meal is a positive, so use that as your base and anything above that is a positive.

Then run the same thought process over the positives. Who do you surround yourself with that influences you for the better in these situations, and what situations do you find yourself in when you experience these positives? Again remember it's how you interpret the experience, not the experience itself, so investigate why you react positively to that person or that situation.

Once you've completed this exercise take some time to assess what areas of your life are generally positive and what areas could use some work, and make a deal with yourself that for the next month you will forget about the negative areas. You won't give them any energy, which means you won't think about them and you won't react to anything that happens in that part of your life during that time and you accept it for what it is. All your focus will be on the positive areas of your life for the next month. Accept, just for a month, that you have no control over the negative areas and just move on with the positives. This is a very powerful exercise but the reason I say do this for a month is that over the first week you will notice a distinct uprising of your negative emotions as they battle for your attention and your survival instinct kicks in. It takes a real level of constant awareness to get through this stage but if you can continue to just accept the negative, and accept that you have no control over it, so therefore it will be what it will be, you will find that into weeks 2 and 3 you will become far less reactive and far less emotive about experiences you have in your life.

Try it now and keep a journal of your emotions and thoughts over the next month.

Soul
The Sixth Step on the Journey....

The Warrior Code

During my lifetime, being born in the 60's, being a kid in the 70's, a teenager in the 80's and beyond, there has been a distinct change in the way young men are educated. When I say educated, in this sense I mean emotional education, how society 'expects' a young man to be.

Every generation believes the generation after it is worse off. The older we get the better we were. In the 60's with the hippie and peace movement, the previous generation had been through the great depression and the second world war, and you could imagine the angst this caused when their children were growing their hair, and smoking pot……..but the world got through it and moved on.

My parents were young teenagers during the Second World War and were young adults during the economic boom of the 1950's. In their lifetime television was introduced and in the 80's the complaint was we always spent too much time inside watching TV, not like when they were young………but we got through.

And now I see it today, my generation looking at the next generation with social media and the internet keeping everyone connected like never before. Not like in our day! We were tougher, we were better…………..but they'll get through.

My point is that every generation is different and it is difficult for the previous generation to accept that they themselves were ever young and did things that their parents didn't like. I am never one to criticise the next generation, after all who has brought up the next generation and taught them how to behave.......we did of

> *Every generation thinks they were better than the next.*
>
> *JR*

course. In every generation fads come and go, technology increases and offers different experiences for new generations, and the lives of each generation are becoming exponentially different to those of the generation before.

But there is one critical element of how every man should or could live their life that is consistent to every generation in history, but that few seem to grasp. It is something spoken about by people from Aurelius' to Ali, from Aristotle to Arnold, from Musashi to Lee, but that is never directly taught and is too often taken completely out of context, and that is living your life by a Warrior Code.

Before we articulate what the Warrior Code is we need to understand what a warrior is, because this is the key element that has been lost over time. Today the term warrior is used in the simple fighting sense, pure aggression and a win at all cost attitude. Nothing markets this term in modern times more than the UFC.

Now beware, I am going off on a rant here.......the warrior typified by the UFC, could not be further from the true attributes of the warrior code. When I say this many scoff and suggest that if you can't fight you can't be called a warrior................ all that does is highlight the small mindedness and lack of warrior attributes they have. The complete and utter lack of respect for your opponent, the arrogance of the winners and the 'look for blame' attitude of the losers sends an incredibly poor picture to young men of what constitutes a true warrior. It's often said there is only one thing worse than a bad loser, and that is a bad winner, but unfortunately that seems to be what sells tickets. Now I am not saying every UFC fighter is a mindless thug, there are the odd one such as Georges St-Pierre who reflect true warrior attributes, but they seem to be in the minority……………....ok Rant over.

Anyone who has read Myomoto Musashi's Book of 5 Rings, will begin to understand the true nature of a Warrior. A warrior does not necessarily have to be the best fighter in the room, otherwise that means there is only one warrior, the biggest and strongest. Being a Warrior is a whole of life attitude, it covers, Mind, Body, Soul and Life.

It's not a coincidence that the basis of my book is around these four pillars. I have been involved in Martial Arts for much of my life to date and I have seen many, many warriors who display attitudes that rank them very highly. I've also seen the guy who has 20 fights under his belt, is hardened and can beat everyone in the gym, but who complains that he doesn't get the recognition he deserves.

We all know what the virtues of a Warrior are, we hear them every day, we see them in inspirational posters, they are espoused by coaches and teachers consistently………….but they get lost. Our society's win at all cost attitude has become a reflection of who we are as a society and as individuals. If we don't win we are a loser. Only warriors are happy. It's pounded into us every day through television and social media. We all love a winner, but that has grown to become an expectation that if we don't win we have lost.

But at the other end of the scale is one of the greatest injustices you can impart on a young man, and that is to teach them to accept mediocrity for excellence. The 'every child is a winner' attitude does nothing to teach young men to be warriors, and young girls to be resilient and self-driven. A warrior must know how to lose and keep moving forward, to lose without having the loss be a reflection of who he is as a man.

The Warrior Code is espoused in many different cultures, in many different ways, through many different actions. The old Knights Code of Chivalry, the Book of 5 Rings, the 7 Virtues of Bushido, the Toa of Jeet Kune Do, and others. They all say the same thing in a different way and they are all centred on core attributes that make a warrior.

So have we established what a warrior is? No not yet. We've established what a warrior is not, and that is they are not a single focused being who is capable of physically defending themselves, that is the distortion of the term.

My version of the Warrior Code is a reflection of all of the great ways of life from history, filtered through my own life experiences, and I have set it in a format that reflects how a Man should live his life in modern society.

Old Boys Warrior Code

- Duty
- Honour
- Judgement
- Tenacity
- Courage

- Belief
- Altruism
- Enterprise

DUTY

As society's freedoms have grown and we have become more and more connected over the last 100 years, society's focus has shifted from responsibilities to rights. Everyone has rights and they should be respected but every individual also has responsibilities and it is to the detriment of society and the individual when rights become more important than responsibilities.

There are 'core' rights that are enshrined and should be respected by all, and fought for if that is what is needed, but it is a small list –

- The right to food
- The right to shelter
- The right to health care
- The right to an education
- The right to freedom of speech

Anything outside these core rights become wants and desires. Immediately I hear some people complaining and starting to list all sorts of other rights, and I don't deny that individuals see different kinds of rights as untouchable, but what are we trying to achieve here?

What we are striving for as Old Boys is to live a meaningful life, live a strong life, live a full life. Anything more than the basic right to exist, tips into desires and wants, and these are subject to your attitude and a multitude of things not in your control, and when these wants and desires (rights) become more important than your responsibilities you become a victim. You look for people to blame, you look for reasons outside the self as to why your rights are not being respected.

I watched a story on the news last week where a middle aged man was taking a court action against the department of housing because they had not provided him a house and he was living on the street with his wife and two kids. The right to shelter is a core right and should be respected and fought for…………………..BUT…………………it was revealed this man had received 5 previous homes from the department of housing and within 12 months had destroyed each house to the point they were unliveable. Where in all this was his responsibility to respect the dwelling he had been given and keep it in a neat and tidy state. Even a Core Right is trumped by Responsibility. It doesn't matter what level of right you are given you have to respect the fact you have been afforded that right.

Yet on the other hand I read a story of a women who owned a café somewhere in America. She was approached one day by a homeless man who asked her for money. Most of us would walk by, some of us would give some coins to avoid any further confrontation. This lady however said to the man, if I give you money you have to give me something in return. If you come to my café tomorrow to wash dishes, clean floors, etc. I will pay you. The lady left and did not expect to see the man again however the next day when she turned up at 4am to set up for the morning shift, there was the homeless man waiting by the door. No doubt she was a little nervous but she allowed the man in and showed him some tasks to do.

Around 10am she was leaving the store for errands and went to the man who had done quite a good job and gave him some money. She thanked him and said if you want to come back tomorrow we can do this again. The man thanked her and she left.

She came back to the coffee shop at 4pm to close up for the day. As soon as she walked in her duty manager came to her and asked about the man she had hired that morning. She immediately thought he may have stolen something or done something bad, but was shocked to hear that he was still there. He had cleaned the kitchen, he had fixed a broken chair, he had swept the path out the front, he had even re-potted the flowers at the front of the shop to make them look better. She was stunned into silence. When she approached the man she asked him why he was still here and he told her that in his recent history no one had ever given him the opportunity to work, to provide for himself and he felt a responsibility to do everything he could to thank her and to grasp this small opportunity to lift himself off the floor.

That was 3 years ago and that man still works for the lady. He is a duty manager and continues to work above and beyond.

This is not a made up story for the purpose of this book. This man went to prison for 5 years for breaking and entering. When he left jail no one, understandably, would give him a job. The system gave him no 'Rights'. But when the smallest of opportunities tapped him on the shoulder he didn't see the need for food and shelter as a right, he only saw his responsibility required to maintain that right, the responsibility he needed to take for his own actions. This man was a genuine victim, but if he maintained the victim mentality then he would still be on the streets.

This man was the living embodiment of having a Warrior Spirit and living the Warrior Code.

HONOUR

Honour, often referred to as Integrity, can be described a simply as –

- Doing the right thing when no one is watching
- Making the right decision when there is no personal gain
- Doing what needs to be done despite the impact on your person.

Honour however has an added ingredient. It means all of the above but to me it also means two other things that are important in a warrior's life –

- Be a gracious loser and (probably the most important)
- Be an Honourable winner

Living with Honour means understanding there is no winning or losing in life, there is only life, and that it is not the end result that is important, but the intent with which you took action, that counts.

We make decisions all day every day. From what to eat for dinner, to how to deal with a problem at work. What clothes to wear to a job interview, to whether I should follow my dream or not. Big decisions, little decisions, life changing decisions.

Living with Honour does not mean making the right decision every time, it means making the decision that is right despite personal gain or loss, and then accepting whatever comes from that decision, good or bad, with grace and honour.

Some people espouse these various Life Virtues as having to live a life of austerity, a life whereby you always put others before yourself. That is such a pessimistic view. Remember what I said before, it is the **intent** with which you made a decision and took action that counts.

If the intent is to get an advantage over someone else to their detriment, then that is not an honourable decision. If the intent is to help yourself and that comes at no disadvantage to someone else then that is an honourable decision.

Let me clarify what I mean by intent. If you make a decision that does not disadvantage you but helps someone else, well that can be honourable, but it can also be dishonourable. If you wouldn't have made that decision if it would have disadvantaged you, then the intent is all about your outcome, and that it is not an honourable decision. Only you in your heart know the real intent of the decisions you make. You can tell the world how great you are, but you will always know the real intent in your heart.

You can most definitely make right decisions and live an honourable life that will see you succeed financially. The two are not mutually exclusive. In fact if you live honourably the more you gain the more you can afford to help others and live an honourable life.

Remember, the essence of the Warrior is to win. But to win without Honour is not acceptable to the true Warrior.

JUDGEMENT

Judgement has two different connotations, external and internal judgement. External judgement is the judgement of other people or situations, the slavery to automatic thoughts and preconceived ideas. Internal judgement is the judgement of oneself, the perception of who we are in the world and how external people and situations impact on us.

When we engage in External Judgement we are again emphasising our primal Fight or Flight instinct. The tendency to judge others is a reflection of our subconscious wanting to be better than those around us, stronger than those around us, and to be right and others wrong. When we are better, stronger, and right, we will survive and thrive over the others. Take a moment to really think about this. What are the real base reasons we judge others? What makes us right and others wrong? Judging others can also be an attempt to be accepted into the group. This is a core reason people join religions, to be right and to have that version of their world accepted and validated by others. Being part of a pack makes us stronger.

Judging others can only make us weaker by limiting our view of the world. It only causes stress because when we have a limited view of what is right and wrong, we will then see everything and everyone in the world that does not agree with our view, and we have no control over what others think or do. If we judge and cannot change the situation, all that does is create stress and anger.

Stop judging other people or situations. This doesn't mean you have to agree with everything you see and hear that does not fit with your values and beliefs, but your values and beliefs are YOUR values and beliefs, not anyone else's, and when you stop judging others by your view of the world, your level of stress and anxiety will begin to dissolve.

Internal judgement is the judgement we place on ourselves. We compare ourselves to others. Judge ourselves by what we perceive are the expectations of society. It's that voice in our heads that keeps putting us down, telling us we aren't good enough, feeling discontent with your lot in life.

Internal judgement is the root cause of stress and anxiety because we are living our lives by the rules of others. It is a desire to be accepted in the group, a need to be wanted and loved, because without that acceptance who are we?

To live the Warrior Code means removing judgement from our way of thinking but often people only think of judgement in the external sense. It is however most important to remove the internal judgement as a priority. You cannot remove the external judgement of people if you do not first remove the internal judgement of yourself. Accept yourself for who you are. Accept that when you try and fail, you have at least tried. Accept the fact you procrastinated and didn't try as hard as you should have, but do not be content with this. We never get life 100% right and in fact if you are getting anywhere above 50% right then you are probably not trying hard enough.

TENANCITY

Tenacity in its simplest form means never give up, but it needs a level of clarification, and as such I call it **WISE TENANCITY**.

Never giving up is a great attribute, and hence why it has made my Warrior Code, but there is a balance between two extremes that must be continually consciously monitored. On the one hand you may be taking certain actions to achieve a goal but

> *If you continue to do what you've always done, you'll continue to get what you've always got.*

you continually miss the mark, but you don't give up and you try again, and again, and again, without ever changing the actions or the way you do things. This is the classic 'If you continue to do what you've always done, you'll continue to get what you've always got'.

At the other extreme you try but miss the mark so you change your actions, then you change them again, then again. In effect you are not being tenacious, you are changing your actions without having put in enough time and effort to see if they actually work and you are using the change of actions as an excuse not to be tenacious and work hard.

The very sad and unfortunately most common trait though is that of taking no action at all. So many people go through life without taking any action, without showing any level of tenacity. They expect things to happen for them with little or no effort. They believe they have a 'right' to be successful without the 'responsibility' of tenacity. These people are driven by a fear of failure and if they make no decisions or take no action or show no tenacity then they can never make a mistake or be disappointed.

Being wisely tenacious is a skill that needs to be developed. You have to live consciously, be aware of what you are doing and what the results are. You will know in your own heart if you have tried hard and when it is time to change actions to achieve a better result.

Sun Tzu's The Art of War talks about this very fact, about how a wise retreat in the face of odds that are stacked against you may lose the battle but ultimately win the war. Be smart, not just brave – be Wisely Tenacious.

> *Do or do not*
> *…..there is no Try.*
>
> **Yoda**

As the great sage Yoda once said – "Do or do not….there is no try"

COURAGE

Courage is an overused word in modern society, so much so it has lost its meaning. Modern media is constantly on the search for more and more extreme 'news', and as they run out of adjectives to describe the same things in a different way, they begin to promote mediocrity as excellence.

So what does courage mean in the context of the Warrior Code. Courage is facing adversity and showing wise tenacity, without losing sight of your values and beliefs. It is not simply about facing a physical foe, it is about facing mental, emotional, and physical challenges with dignity, while maintaining self-respect and respect for others.

One thing courage is <u>NOT</u>, is acting on your responsibilities. We've spoken about how as a Warrior your Responsibilities take precedence over your Rights. This is the opposite to the general expectation of society that goes to great lengths to fight for their rights, but pays no dues to the responsibilities that come with those rights. You have a responsibility to treat people with respect. A responsibility to be a good citizen. A responsibility to your employer. It is not courageous to act on these responsibilities. No matter what story you tell yourself, your responsibilities are not courageous, they are a baseline for living the Warrior Code.

Physical courage is the most easily understood. The courage a soldier faces in battle is primal. To be able to keep your wits when you are faced with imminent danger is a special trait.

Another example of Physical Courage is being faced with a threat from another person or persons, to you and your family. Being able to stand and fight to protect your loved ones, despite the odds, is courageous.

But fighting in and of itself is not all there is to being courageous. Just because you can fight does not automatically make you courageous.

Principled Courage is standing up for what you believe in despite those about you disagreeing with or laughing at your stance. But let's be very clear here…….I said above that courage is facing challenges and adversity <u>whilst maintaining self-respect and respect for others</u>.

Terrorists believe they are courageous because they will die for their beliefs and take as many lives of innocent people with them as possible. This is not courage.

How many demonstrations do you see where a group of people are fighting for their rights and standing up for their beliefs, but they preach hate against those that disagree with their view. This is not courage.

A great example of Principled Courage was Mahatma Ghandi. Ghandi was discriminated against in South Africa and driven out of the country only to return to his homeland India where he lead the struggle for self-rule against the British, yet he has always maintained a stance of non-violence, and always showed respect to the British.

Emotional courage is the least recognised of all the forms of courage, yet I believe is the greatest. This is the courage to face your own demons. The courage to own up to your own weaknesses and to fight to change for the better. This type of courage is evident in everyday life yet we call it stress, anxiety and depression. The personal courage to constantly fight to be a better person sums up what the Warrior Code is all about.

As the great philosopher Rocky Balboa once said, "It's not how hard you can hit, it's how hard you can get hit and keep moving forward".

BELIEF

Belief in yourself is one of the keys to living a full and satisfied life. The opposite of self-belief is doubt, anxiety, fear of what 'they' will say, and fear of failure. Unfortunately though most people talk a great game about belief in themselves and bugger what all the others say, but when it boils down to them and their own thoughts, they are filled with fear and self-doubt.

To have self-belief does not mean you get things right, it means you try, fail, adjust course, and re-try, but to keep this cycle moving forward you have to be in tune with your core values, understand what you want in life. Remember that what you truly want in life is not materialistic things…..what you really want is how those materialistic things will make you feel. Belief in the emotions you want to feel, and the type of person you want to be….a Warrior….is what it's all about.

The greatest hurdle to self-belief is the nay-sayers. Whenever you try something that is different from the crowd you will get many more people tell you it can't be done, or who will talk behind your back about how silly that is or how stupid you

> *The ability to maintain self-belief in the face of negativity is one of the greatest achievements you can make in your life.*
>
> **JR**

are. The reason these people do this is because they don't want to be seen to be different from the crowd, it's a survival mechanism. You must remember this is their weakness not yours. The ability to maintain self-belief in the face of negativity is one of the greatest achievements you can make in your life, and will open up an amazing world of possibility.

ALTRUISM

Being Altruistic should be a simple concept to understand but is often lost in translation. As a Warrior, to be seen to be Altruistic is the opposite of the true meaning. Altruism is a personal journey, as are all the characteristics of the Warrior Code, and is not a means for seeking gratification or gain. There are people who are wealthy and successful and give large amounts to charities and also make sure people know they did. This is often done for materialistic as well as gratification gain. But so also are there people who are average citizens who do things to help others in need, but they also make sure others know. They want to be seen as great people. I saw many of these on Sunday at church, growing up as a good catholic boy!

Being successful and wealthy is not mutually exclusive to being altruistic. Take a look at Bill and Melinda Gates. The wealthiest people on the planet. The charities they have set up and operate with the absolute goal of making the world a better place, are amazing, and they seek no personal gain. Now I hear you say, but that's easy if you have Billions of dollars. Well yes it is easier to set up a world wide fund to support vaccination of children in Africa, but that's not the point. The homeless man who helps an old lady across the road, is as altruistic as Bill Gates, for he is doing what he can with what he has.

There is another misnomer that comes with being altruistic, that is that it should not make you feel happy and good. Why on earth would I continue to do things for others if they made me feel bad about myself? The Dalai Lama has said that he has selfish reasons for showing empathy and being altruistic, it makes him feel good.

Remember it is not the act itself on which altruism is judged, it is the intent behind the act. Are you doing it so others will say how good you are? Or are you doing it simply because it is the right thing to do and it makes you a better person?

ENTERPRISE

Enterprise is wholly living. It's living adventurously. It's getting every experience out of life that is possible. Enterprise is opening yourself up to new experiences, living in the moment and accepting outcomes good and bad, because it is the experience that is the goal, not the result. It is how life makes you feel that is the true purpose of your life, not how many toys you have or how much money you accumulate.

Try things, have experiences, live in the moment, try, fail, adjust and retry.

Enterprise is about making decisions and taking action, but this does not simply apply to the big decisions in life, it also applies to the very small, and in fact it is the very small decisions that we often make sub-consciously or make based on habit or automatic thought, that lead us to the places where the big decisions are made.

We all have choice at every juncture of the day. A decision is a fork in the pathway of our life that takes us in a certain direction. These 'forks in the road' happen all day every day but the problem is we generally take no notice. We make the small decisions without thinking, we make them based on what we have always done, what is easy. Yet every decision leads you on a new path, and that path changes direction exponentially based on the decisions we make, and by the time we reach a major intersection where a big decision is required we finally become conscious of what we are deciding on, and for the first time we stop looking at our feet and lift our heads to see where we are, and we realise we are lost and a long way from home.

We make one decision and head on a path that then leads to another decision and the path splits again, and again, and again. Eventually, if we are not conscious of the little decisions, our life can be so far from where we wanted to be that we cannot see any way back.

But if we make all the little decisions consciously and in line with our core values, then when we get to the big decisions we find it is a place we always dreamt of, and when we look back we can't believe how far we have come and how much better we are as a person than who we used to be.

TASK

Values & Meanings

It is not enough to know the Warrior Code and understand its principles, it must be lived. That is what it is all about, living a life worth living. But to do this you first must understand your core values and beliefs because without this understanding you are simply making random decisions based on what feels good at the time. I refer you back to the first pillar **MIND and its Second Step on The Journey – Core Value Beliefs**. You will find in here the direction to discovering your Core Value Beliefs that will act as the map on your life journey.

Soul
The Seventh Step on the Journey....

The Middle Way

There is a strong theme that runs through Buddhism that provides a way of living, thinking, and acting. It is referred to as the Middle Way and is something that is worth the effort to study and understand.

The Middle Way is about recognising extremes of thought and behaviour and understanding that extremes of anything only lead to rigid outcomes, stress and anxiety. It is about the Acceptance of what is, and the understanding that the only thing you truly have control of in your life is how you react to the things that you experience every day.

The original Buddhist concept was to compare the ascetic life of a Monk who starves himself, abstains from any pleasures whatsoever, and treads the stringent and extreme monastic life in search of fulfilment and happiness. As compared to the indulgent and materialistic life of the wealthy and influential whose search for happiness lies in the acquisition of material possessions. Buddha lead both lifestyles, starting out as a wealthy prince, then leading an extreme monastic life, only to come to the conclusion that neither way brings true happiness and peace, but rather the Middle Way is where these things are to be found. The search for meaning is not found in extremes.

Understand that this does not apply to extremes of effort. It does not mean we accept mediocrity for excellence, and in fact far from it. It does not take away from our Responsibilities nor does the Middle Way correspond to the Easy Way.

Let's take the example of an elite athlete, or a successful businessman. Both these people are reaching for what the average Joe might consider extremes, but what they are reaching for is their full potential. Our life should be about reaching for our full potential. Walking the Middle Way is not in contrast to 'striving for excellence' and in fact it is completely aligned and is an amazing tool in helping you achieve the best you can be.

With a striving for excellence can often come stress and anxiety as we judge ourselves against the performance of others or judge ourselves against the expectations of ourselves. It can be easy when striving for your full potential to enter into extremes of thought or action which lead to stress and anxiety. How many times when striving for a goal do you see people either accept nothing less than 100% achievement as successful, or they give up at the first sign of failure. The Middle Way teaches us to recognise when we have gone too far off the path and reminds us to focus on what is important and what we can control. It reminds us to lift our head up every now and then and see where we are and make sure we are seeing the bigger picture and that the way ahead is clear.

This original concept can be utilised in every area of our life. It reminds us that there are two sides to every story and that strongly held opinions more often than not reflect a defence mechanism that is seeking acceptance and love, rather than being built on principle. Be careful with having stringent 'Principles', that having these principles does not mean you have become intolerant or unwilling to accept that there may be other ways in which people see the world that are as genuine and acceptable as your own. This is the Middle Way.

It can be difficult to understand and reconcile how The Middle Way works with striving to achieve goals, but when you do it opens up an amazing way of striving for goals that allows you to accept setbacks without having them destroy your confidence. It allows you to celebrate achievements without thinking the job is done, and reminds you to control the controllables and let the rest go.

The Middle Way reminds you that the Journey is the Goal, not the Goal. Taking action towards being a better person physically, emotionally, and spiritually is what is important. The outcomes are what they will be.

TASK:

Take it upon yourself to do some research on The Middle Way. It espouses much of what this whole Journey of life is about and will help you understand many of the recurring themes in this book.

Soul
The Eighth Step on the Journey....

The Backyard Buddhist

I am no spiritual guru, I am no psychotherapist, and I am no Dalai Lama, but I do consider I have a few experiences, some education, a bit of life experience, and a burning desire to share my thoughts about life with others in the hope I may make a difference, no matter how small, in someone's life.

I consider myself a Backyard Buddhist.

Being a Backyard Buddhist encompasses all the themes discussed in this section on SOUL. It's about living consciously. Conscious of your actions and their outcomes. It's a life where your responsibilities are more important than your rights. It's a life where you live your life's purpose…not someone else's.

This concept of being a Backyard Buddhist means living life to its fullest, being open to new experiences, being tolerant, and accepting of the things you do not control. It is not a life of extreme action on things that are not aligned to our core values, as this leads to burnout or stress when our outcomes are impacted by the things we cannot control. The classic example of this is climbing the corporate ladder. We work long hours and we work under pressure to provide for ourselves and our family in the future. Being a Backyard Buddhist does not mean we don't have to do these things, we have to, that's just life. I spent 20 years trying to climb the corporate ladder, and I'm still trying hard to provide for me and my family. But a Backyard Buddhist faces these challenges with understanding of what they can and can't do, what they control and what they can't control, and they accept the outcomes of their actions good or bad. They remove stress by doing the best they can with what they have and accepting whatever the outcome may be.

A Backyard Buddhist does not live a life of extreme opinion. Don't be so fixated on being right. Stop thinking you have to defend who you are or what you stand for, people will disagree with you regardless of what you say or think, believe it or not, it doesn't make them wrong, and it doesn't make them right, it is simply them defending their own version of themselves. Extreme opinions have a tendency to lead to ignorance and intolerance, and it becomes a vicious circle of defence, attack, and harden your position ready for the next attack. The whole world today has become significantly less tolerant and far more opinionated. Partially economically driven (the GFC), and partially religiously driven (Terrorism), the world has taken a decided leap into the extreme opinion and defence of the self. We could do with a lot more Backyard Buddhists!

> *Do your best, with what you have, where you are, and accept whatever the outcome may be....*
>
> *JR*

Act of Random Kindness (ARK)

It is very difficult to say I am not going to be negative, I am not going to be opinionated, I am going to accept whatever happens. You know why these are hard? It's because you are trying to NOT do something. You are focusing on the problem, and

> *Just do a single ARK every day and don't tell anyone you did it. See how it changes you.*
>
> *JR*

what you focus on is what your world becomes.

A Backyard Buddhist does not try to stop being anything, they simply try to be something better. One very simple and very powerful way of starting the journey of change is to perform one ARK every day. An ARK can be as simple as holding the door open for someone you don't know to walk through, tell someone they have done well, check on someone to make sure they are ok. The power of this is phenomenal. How it makes you feel is amazing. They are small acts but the key is you are conscious of having done something good, something that makes you a better person.

The power of focusing on being a better person, rather than focusing on not being a negative person, is the key to where it all starts. Focus on strengths, and weaknesses will take care of themselves.

TASK:

For the next 6 weeks do at least one ARK every day. Write them down at the end of every day in your journal. Keep them small and simple it doesn't need to be grand gestures, and most importantly don't tell anyone what you are doing. This is all about you being a better person…..not about getting other people to think you are a better person.

Soul
The Ninth Step on the Journey....

Tools to Help You Achieve

Becoming a better person and realising your life's purpose does not come easily. Setting goals and taking actions are 50% of the requirements. The other 50% requires you to live consciously. You must be constantly aware of your actions, aware of situations and people you surround yourself with, and be constantly aware of your thoughts, and most importantly constantly aware of your automatic thoughts and actions that will do their best to sabotage your progress without you even realising it.

There are many tools available but most can be compiled into 4 distinct categories –

- Affirmations
- Visualisation
- Meditation
- Breathing Techniques

Affirmations

So right up front....I hate affirmations. I think they are the biggest falsehood that has ever been dispensed into the personal development industry. I say this primarily because affirmations are such an easy cop out and they are the most misunderstood of all the tools.

You see this all the time, *"Tell yourself 10 times every morning that today will be a great day"...."Keep repeating to yourself I am a good person"*. This is shallow and meaningless for 99% of ordinary people in the world.

Now I'm not saying you wake up and continue your old patterns of thinking how bad this day will be, or telling yourself you are useless. Obviously negative self-talk is bad, but let's be real, it's hard not to be negative sometimes. There is so much in the world you can't control, so many people who don't have the same perception of the world that you do, that you constantly feel like you have to fight for your place at the table. Don't ignore that, it's the way life is. But what have we been saying throughout this journey? There is only one thing you can control and that is how you think, behave, and react. That's it......nothing else.

The problem with affirmations is that the way they are taught a majority of the time lacks the teaching of 'Core Beliefs' and 'Acceptance of What Is'. If you get up in the morning and repeat 10 times, "Today will be a great day....today will be a great day.....today will be a great day...etc." and you really feel the emotion and believe it to be true, that's great. But what happens when you get to work and your boss is immediately onto you about why that report hasn't been finished? If you are not able to know that you have done the best you could on that report (lived your core beliefs and values), and able to accept the boss's criticism no matter how ill-founded (acceptance of what is), then your day has all of a sudden turned to crap.

Tony Robbins, one of the greatest personal development gurus of all time, has a favourite saying about this. He talks about your garden and you continually affirm *"There are no weeds in my garden....there are no weeds in my garden.....there are no weeds in my garden"*, and you truly believe, feel and see it……………makes absolutely no difference if you don't take action. This sounds obvious but the same principle applies to the intangible situation of affirming you will have a great day but you have taken no action to be able to accept the things you can't control and to live by your core beliefs. Words are empty without action and core beliefs that align with who you really want to be.

TASK

Remember what we learnt in **MIND – Step 2 of the Journey** about Core Beliefs and Values? Go back and study this section. It is the core of being able to live a stress free life.

Also review **MIND – Step 6 of the Journey**, the Myth of Control, just to remind yourself about the Acceptance of What Is, and controlling the controllables

Day Dreaming (Visualisation)

Visualisation (as it's called by most of the experts) is a very strong tool but one that is significantly harder to master. There are many studies that confirm your body and brain cannot distinguish between what is physically happening and what is imagined, if they are both conducted with feeling and true belief. The famous saying 'What you think, you become' is the core of visualisation.

I have used visualisation throughout my life, albeit I didn't realise what I was actually doing at first. I remember first using visualisation in my martial arts. I would have a grading coming up and I was trying to master various Katas or routines. I would lie in

> *What you think you become.*

bed at night imagining and feeling myself going through the Kata step by step. I would do this until I fell asleep. I wasn't trying to practice visualisation, I was simply trying to make sure I didn't stuff up on the day. Potential embarrassment is a strong motivator!

What has always amazed me about this is the visualisation I completed on my Katas had an incredibly strong influence even overnight. There were obvious changes day to day, in how much more of my Kata I remembered each day when I physically tried to do it.

Of course that is visualisation in its simplest and easiest form. The challenge is to transfer this mind-body connection to intangible areas of your life. How can we visualise improving our own well-being, or reducing anxiety, or striving to achieve a goal? This is where the real benefits are to be gained. I know visualisation works, but it is a difficult practice. There are many ways to visualise and many practices make it a very formal meditative thing that should be done in a certain way at a certain time each day. This never worked for me, it felt like I was trying too hard. My form of visualisation would be better described as day dreaming. I like to do my visualisation when I am in bed and as I am drifting off to sleep. At that time I feel less prone to being distracted, and I feel more amenable to thinking openly.

Let's take for example my goal to write this book, to share my thoughts with other people. The biggest issue for me, and what caused me to delay this writing process for many years, was a deep seated fear of what others would think or say, but once I started to day dream about what it would be like to complete a book, the sense of achievement, the feeling that I had actually achieved something meaningful with my life, the process started to take shape. I was more confident to make a start, and to keep working on my goal a little bit every day. And the more I visualised the more my confidence grew, and the more feeling and realistic my day dreams became. Visualisation is all about identifying the feelings that the goal will give you and let yourself feel them. It's not about visualising the new car you want, it's about identifying how that car will make you feel when you have it. It's not the tangible goal, it's the emotional goal that's important.

But beware, day dreaming is a double edged sword. Just as it can produce good positive outcomes, so can it enhance negative feelings. We all know that person who is negative all the time. They are the classic glass half empty kind of person. You can guarantee that their day dreaming is always about what could go wrong, never what might go right.

Now changing from thinking negatively to thinking positively is no easy task, but it is something you need be very conscious of. With all the negativity in the world and in the media that surrounds us 24/7, it is very easy to be dragged into negative thinking. This is why I find Day Dreaming better than Visualisation. To me visualisation is something you are trying to do, it's something you have to work at, and can become a chore and as such reinforces some negative facets of your mind. Day dreaming to me is relaxed, with no expectations or preconceived outcomes. I like just sitting back and thinking "wouldn't it be nice if…" and then just let my mind wander for a while. As soon as a negative thought creeps in I don't try to ignore it, as that just leads to tension, I accept it and think about how I would work through that if it happened. Day dreaming becomes a fun journey and with that it is far easier to stay positive.

TASK

Take a close look at your thoughts. When you are alone and relaxed, what does your mind drift to? Are you easily distracted by negative thoughts? Becoming conscious of where your mind is at is important. Don't be led by your mind. You need to guide your mind to where you want it to be.

Tonight when you go to bed, lie down with your eyes closed and think about something you would like to achieve or a place you would like to visit and just day dream about what it would be like to achieve this thing. Feel the sensations, hear the noises, and engage with your emotions. If while you are thinking, a negative thought enters your head like 'This is stupid I will never achieve this', accept that thought and say 'Well maybe I won't achieve it, but just for a few minutes I'm going to imagine I have'.

This technique of Day Dreaming can take time to get used to but by being relaxed and allowing yourself to not be bound by any preconceived ideas or restricted by negative thoughts, it can become a very fulfilling way to finish the day, and over time will have an amazing effect on your attitude, confidence and ability to see your goals much clearer.

Yoga Meditation

Meditation and Yoga were once something that was the domain of the Buddhist Monk, or the Nimbin Hippie, but no longer. Meditation had always been something I had tried but kept it to myself and made sure I did it in the dark when no one was watching. That was until 2006 when I travelled to Thailand to attend a Muay Thai camp and train for a month. It was at this camp that I finally felt I could 'come out of the closet' as a meditation practitioner, when I saw that the professional fighters at the camp all had to attend Yoga and Meditation each morning. All of a sudden it felt ok.

Now it shouldn't have taken that experience for me to accept myself as a Yogi or Meditator, but that's the era I grew up in, during the 70's and 80's in country Australia, when there was obviously something seriously wrong with you if you engaged in those heretic eastern practices.

I can say now that yoga and meditation have been a wonderful thing not only for peace of mind and reducing my stress levels, but have proven an amazing tool for longevity in my martial arts practices.

Note I call this topic 'Yoga Meditation' not 'Yoga and Meditation'. For me they are not two separate things. I confess I have always found deep meditation hard. After much practice I was able to enter a thought-free state for short periods but I always felt it was hard work, even though the whole point of meditation is that you stop striving, stop trying, just be. What I discovered in Thailand was the practice of Yoga combined with Meditation. All of a sudden things changed for me. My mind or my body needed something to focus on and Yoga proved to be that thing. In meditation there are many tools that you can focus on including the breathing, a Mandala, or a specific sound or word. These are all meant to stop the voice in your head from incessantly thinking and talking. Yoga was my Mandala. I have since developed my own Yoga Meditation practice that really works for me. It allows me to concentrate on the pose or the stretch whilst breathing in a slow rhythm or cadence.

But one thing I strongly encourage you to do is experiment. There is no right or wrong way to do this, I don't care what the experts say. Anyone who says this is the way you must meditate is completely missing the point of meditation in the first place. Meditation is a state, not an action, and every person is different and as such will have different ways of attaining that state. Sure, don't hesitate to get some instruction so you have the basics right, that is just common sense, but you will know when you are ready to change things to your own style. It's exactly the same as Martial Arts. I've seen so many Martial Artists train to get their Black Belt with some idea that once they achieve the coveted Black Belt they will all of a sudden be taught the deeply held secrets of the Masters. So many are disappointed to realise that they are the same person they were before and that the Five Finger Death Punch isn't real….. although it was very effective in Kill Bill.

The point is you study and practice the basics. As in Martial Arts, there are basics to be learnt in Yoga and Meditation, so don't think you know it all, make sure you understand the basics, but once you are competent (have your Black Belt) its then that it is time to start your own journey, Experiment for yourself and understand what works for you and why it works for you and why other ways work for others.

Breathing Techniques

Breathing techniques are numerous. There are many techniques and methods of utilising a focus on the breath for meditation and overall health. I am a strong advocate of breathing techniques as they are something you can do even when in a crowd of people or standing in front of an audience, that are not noticeable to others, but can provide huge and immediate benefit to you.

Through my Martial Arts I have researched and developed my own breathing techniques but the first time I remember using breathing to calm my self was when I was 17. I was the Vice-Captain of the Boarding School I attended and part of that role required giving various speeches and representing the college at functions and events, and generally taking a leadership role. Now speaking in front of an audience was akin to being in a horror movie for me…it scared the crap out of me to the point where I even found it hard to get the first words out.

The first time I felt the impact of a breathing technique I was to give an address at our Awards night in front of about 1,000 family and students. I was standing behind the stage in a sheer state of panic and genuinely wondering if I could feign some serious illness to get out of it. I was actually starting to hyperventilate and I remember just stopping and trying hard to slow my breathing, deeper and slower, and for 3 breaths I forgot all about what was in front of me and I felt the endorphins kick in as my breathing slowed. At that moment I was called to the podium and I was calm and confident and started to deliver my speech. Half way through though I started to realise where I was and what I was doing and my knees started to shake uncontrollably and the anxiety came back…but I had started and that was the big hurdle out of the way.

I didn't see that moment as practicing any sort of breathing technique, I was just trying not to pass out. But as my Martial Arts career evolved I was exposed to the benefits of various breathing techniques and I grew in my knowledge and application.

One such technique I use often is called Circular Breathing. I use this in emotional stress situations, and also in physical stress situations. The emotional stress situations can be anything similar to what I described above. A good example of the physical stress situation is as follows.

I had 6 kickboxing fights early on with an average 4 wins 2 loss record. I loved it and was ok at it but also realised I was never going to be a world beater. Coming into the fight provides an enormous amount of emotional stress, and I don't care how many fights you have had, ask any experienced fighter and it is always there. In fact if you're not a bit nervous, maybe you are not ready. Anyway, I used circular breathing before the start of my fights. But in between rounds you are completely stuffed. Your emotional stress is gone at the end of round 1, it's all now about how you handle the physical stress and how hard you trained prior to the fight that will be the telling factors. In my corner I would enter into 3 circular breathes immediately at the end of the round and 3 just before the start of the next round. This slowing of the breathing assisted with deeper breathing and better oxygen intake, and also helped focus the mind to the present moment. Of course there's nothing better to focus the mind on the present than a straight right hand to the face.

Back in **MIND – The First Step on the Journey** we gave an explanation of the mechanics of Circular Breathing as follows –

To circular breathe, breathe in through the nose and imagine the air is a white light. It passes through your nose and then travels down your spine. As it travels down the spine actually imagine you can feel it lighting the spine up as it moves down. At the bottom of the spine the air/light enters your Dan Tian which is the area between the navel and the groin. In Martial Arts and eastern practices this is considered the centre of the body.

The 4 Pillars of Life

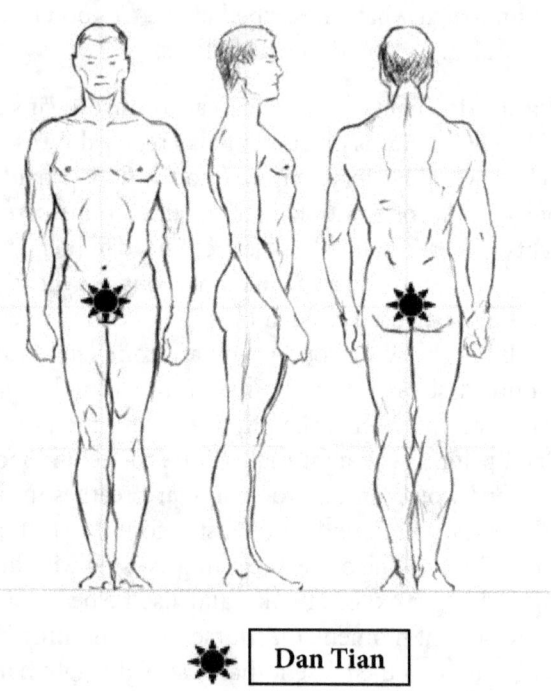

Dan Tian

As the air enters the Dan Tian it begins to fill the area with an expanding light until the lungs are full. Then you start to breathe out through the mouth.

The next step is a tricky part to get used to, but just try. Imagine the breath leaving the mouth is black smoke, all the toxins, and negativity, that is stored in your body, leaving the body. At the same time the light in the Dan Tian expands into all parts of the body to replace this 'black smoke'.

Once you have taken one 'Circular Breath' you may find in the first few times you do this that you are puffing a little. This is because by focusing on breathing into the Dan Tian, it is making you breathe to the bottom of your lungs. This is something we rarely do as we tend to breathe shallow and don't use the full capacity of our lungs. After the first circular breath just breathe normally again for a few breathes, and then when you are ready, do another circular breath.

TASK

There are many different techniques to help you achieve your goals and make your way towards a happy and peaceful existence. Open your mind and do your research and eventually you will find a technique or a mixture of different techniques that resonate with the type of person you are.

Soul
The Tenth Step on the Journey....

Nurture V Nature

There has been significant scientific and human behaviour debate over many years about the impact of Nurture V Nature.

Nurture is the way we were brought up, the society we were influenced by, the experiences we have had, and the impacts all of those experiences since our birth have had on the way we think and act now.

Nature is our genetics, what we were born with, the genes our parents gave us, our lineage, and how all these things influence the person we are today.

One of the strongest statements of the power of Nurture that has been made is "give me a child from birth until he is 7 years old and he will be mine for life". Whether this is true or not is open for debate but it is a strong statement on the power of early indoctrination.

Personally I believe, like most things in life, there is no black and white, only shades of grey. Both nature and nurture have an impact, and depending on an individual's psychic make up and their penchant to accept change, then one or the other can have very different impacts.

There are several stories about twins being separated at birth and growing up in very different environments including the level of wealth and attitudes of the adopted parents. What is clearly seen in these cases is that whilst both of them have very different outlooks on life and how the world works, they retain many similarities in terms of the way they process information and their acceptance of change or otherwise.

My own life is an example of this conflict between Nurture V Nature. I have 2 sisters and 1 brother but they are between 10 and 15 years older than me (fairly sure I was a mistake…). My sisters and brother were born and had their early years on cattle properties until my father moved to Cairns for work. My sisters and brother lived at home until they were about 18-20.

When I was 5 years old I moved with my parents to Charleville in western Queensland. My brother and sisters stayed in Cairns as they had left school and were working. As such I was effectively an 'only child'. We then moved around western Queensland a bit until I was 12 years old when I was sent away to Boarding School. My upbringing from then on changed dramatically and went from a small town as an only child with a limited range of influences, to living with 400 other boys 24/7. I lived in this environment during my formative teenage years until I was 17 and I never moved back home. After school I made my own way in the world.

The Nurture V Nature debate in my case can be seen very clearly in certain ways. I think very differently to my siblings in terms of world views and my attitudes to other people and places. Not in a right or wrong way, just different. I am far more outgoing and generally annoying (according to my daughters) than my siblings who are more conservative.

But with all those differences, it is clear to see the impacts of Nature. There are physical looks and habits of course but that is not what I am talking about here. There are core ways that some of my automatic thoughts come to the fore and the way some experiences affect me that are inbuilt in the sense that I have inherited them and they are part of my nature traits.

So the question is, how can you change either the things that you were born with or your past experiences? The first thing is to realise you can't change anything that has happened to you or anything that you were given naturally. The second thing is to stop using that as an excuse for not changing.

It's such an easy excuse to blame your parents, blame an experience from the past, and say there is nothing you can do as it's just the way you are. I know because I did just that for years. I blamed past experiences for my anger issues and for my lack of patience. It was just who I was that caused me to behave inappropriately when confronted with certain situations. It's not easy but it's also not impossible to change. There is a path but there is no quick fix.

The first step is to accept your past, don't fight against it. Accept your Nature traits, and accept the Nurture you were given, no matter how bad. It is what it is and is a part of who you are. It's not what has happened to you, it's how you think and act moving forward.

The second step is to start looking forward. By accepting the past leaves you able to focus on the future. What kind of person do I want to be?

The third step is to really investigate your automatic thoughts and behaviours. When faced with a situation that makes you react angrily, why do you behave the way you do? Really see that the reasons you react in certain ways is not just about the situation in front of you, it is the way you have been conditioned to react through years of experiences. It can be confronting to look so closely at your own reactions, but the key is to stay away from blame. Don't feel you have to defend the way you react, just accept that is what happened in the moment and try to understand why. Being defensive just reinforces the trait.

The fourth step is to live consciously. Once you accept your past, understand why you react the way you do, and then have a vision for who you want to be, then you have to live consciously. By living consciously you take notice of your automatic thoughts and behaviours that reinforce your past, and you are able to identify in the moment what it is doing to your emotions and your own happiness. These thoughts and behaviours are the product of your past and you react to situations with them without even thinking. Hidden in these automatic thoughts are the keys to your happiness. It's not the past that is the problem, it's how you react in the moment.

TASK

Take an emotion that you know you don't like, that makes you behave in certain ways and that you know makes you unhappy. It could be anger, it could be automatically thinking the worst in a situation, or any other thing that impacts your life regularly.

Think about the last time this happened, what happened to trigger your emotion, and how did you react?

Now link that reaction to either a Nurture or Nature issue, it could be a bit of both. Look at your past and investigate where this emotion may have been formed. What did the current situation remind you of from your past? What other situations in the past have triggered that emotion? Start to look for something that happened or from the way some of your relatives may have behaved that may give some explanation to your emotional behaviour.

This process helps to externalise the emotion. It helps to separate the emotion and the way you reacted, from you as a person. It is important to understand that the emotion and its subsequent behaviour are not a reflection of you as a person, they are a reflection of something from your past, an experience or a trait.

Now see and feel how your emotion and behaviour affect your own life, your own happiness, and how it affects the people around you. How would you like that to be different?

Now live consciously. With this investigation into yourself you can now see a different reason for the emotions and your past behaviours. It can be seen as something separate from who you are as a person and now whenever you realise that emotion has taken you over, or you react in a certain way, you will be able to stop and reflect on this and it will help you to move to overcome this emotion. The first few times of living consciously you will go through the whole automatic reaction and subsequent behaviour and only later when you have calmed down will you realise what you just did. That is great. That is living consciously. What happens then as you keep this practice up, is that the time between the start of the emotion and time you become conscious of how you are reacting gets smaller and smaller until eventually you will start to notice situations occurring in front of you that may trigger that emotion, and you are ready for them and hence your behaviour becomes permanently changed for the better.

Soul
The Eleventh Step on the Journey....

Opinions are Overrated

"Opinions are like bums. Whilst everyone has one, some are well trained, tight, and to be admired....... some though are just arseholes." JR

You often hear people say 'you have to have an opinion', or 'what's your opinion'. It seems that you have to have an opinion on everything, just look at the Letters to the Editor in your local paper. There you will see people with all sorts of opinions and feeling the need to have to defend their opinion.

My opinion, is that anyone who has a strong unshakeable opinion, and feels the need to defend that opinion as strongly as they can, is intolerant and insecure. Of course that's just my opinion.......

I'm not saying having an opinion is wrong. It's important to have opinions about values and beliefs, but when you feel the need to defend that opinion and tell someone else they are wrong, then your opinion has all of a sudden become an integral part of how you see yourself as a person, and that leads to intolerance and ignorance. Your opinions should not be 'who you are', they should simply be something you think or believe at this point in time, but that are pliable and open to change and adjustment as you become more educated and more open to the world around you.

Always remember there are two sides to every story and I mean EVERY story. It doesn't matter how strongly you disagree with

> *There are two sides to **EVERY** story.*

the other person, they have a different perception of reality from you. Their reality has been shaped by their life experiences just the same as your life has by your own experiences. What makes them wrong and you right? Always take the time to consider the opinion of someone else and try and put yourself in their shoes and see how they could have come to form their opinion. The ability to see an argument from the others point of view is a fundamental management skill. By being able to see the reasons someone else holds an opinion will allow you to be able to seek solutions that can satisfy their fears or needs. This is a subtle and crucial skill that all great leaders have in their arsenal.

In the Old Boys Warrior Code in Step Six of the Soul Journey we spoke about Rights V Responsibilities. The Right to have Rights comes with Responsibilities that must be fulfilled. Rights are not mutually exclusive from Responsibilities. It's the same with Opinions. Having an Opinion is a Right, but it comes with a Responsibility to ensure your opinion is fair and reasonable, does not negatively impact others, and that you remain open-minded enough to accept that there are other versions of people's personal reality that are as real to them as your opinion is to you. Rights and Opinions that are held without the associated Responsibilities and Open-mindedness only ever lead to inflexibility, intolerance and ignorance.

Now please don't misunderstand me and think that I am talking about being PC (Politically Correct) or some sort of turning the other cheek. Neither of these attributes have a place in a Warriors life.

Being open-minded has nothing to do with being PC. There is a very big difference between not being a racist ignorant bastard, compared to not saying something because it may offend someone or something.

Being a racist ignorant bastard is a choice and is aimed at offending someone or something you don't like. It is the ultimate defence of an opinion.

However not saying something because it may offend someone offers nothing to society or the world. It is important to have values and beliefs and as long as those values and beliefs have positive effects on you and those around you then what is wrong with that opinion? It's when you refuse to try and understand the view or opinion of the other person that you lose.

You also lose if you just 'Turn the other cheek' which is a popular Christian parable. I'm sorry but all that does is reinforce the ignorance of the bully who struck you on the cheek. Don't be afraid to hold your opinion and defend your opinion…..just be careful you don't feel you have to defend your opinion as a means of defending who you are as a person, and that your defence does not turn into an attack on the other persons view of themselves.

> *Turning the other cheek simply reinforces the ignorance of the bully and has no place in a Warriors Life.*
>
> *JR*

TASK:

Think about a view that you hold strongly and where there are others that disagree with you. Politics and Religion are fertile grounds for opinions. Think about the situation and the person who disagrees whole heartedly with you. Step back mentally from the situation and take a look at that other person as if they were a science lab experiment. What makes them tick? What experiences could this person have had in their life that makes them think so differently to you? What is the best outcome that that person's opinion could achieve if it came through?

Try and see the situation from the others perspective. This is a difficult exercise but keep at it. The harder it is for you to see the others view of the world, the more you yourself are tied to your own opinions as to what is right and what is wrong.

Soul
The Twelfth Step on the Journey....

When the going gets tough.....Take smaller steps

The Journey of The Soul can seem to be a complex one, but in reality the simpler you make it the easier it is. Everyone follows a different path, and whilst there are plenty of guides out there to show you the way, always remember you have to cut your own path, not walk someone else's. Too many of us live our lives following someone else's ideas……get out the machete and head off into the bush and cut your own path.

Patience is a virtue…..something you've probably heard your mother say. Patience was unfortunately something I lacked in my younger days and even though I have developed a level of patience in middle age, I still rate poorly on the patience scale. It's a paradox when trying to follow your soul, or find your spiritual path, that the harder you try the further it gets away from you. The more you desire, the more stressed you get. It's a difficult concept to master, that being patient and open minded will achieve more in a quicker time. Our modern western society is all about instant gratification and must have now. But a Soul or Spiritual journey works in exactly the opposite way.

> *Patience is a virtue….I just wish it didn't take so long.*

Of course there will be many times in your life when the going gets tough, no matter how much you accept what you can't control. There will be times when you have shown all the patience in the world and the acceptance of a saint but you reach a stage where you think *"I've had enough…I just want a small win, that's all. Is that too much to ask?"* I know that question very well, I don't know how many times that has crossed my thoughts or even been shouted out loud when I'm in the car alone.

When you reach this stage there is only one answer, take smaller steps but keep moving forward. This is the essence of never giving up. Just because when you started this journey you wanted to achieve a goal by a certain date, but life and the 'uncontrollables' have gotten in the way to prevent you meeting that deadline, doesn't mean you give up. It also doesn't mean you have to power up and work 10 times harder. Both those options just lead to stress, anxiety and burnout, and the goal gets further and further away. It may even have the effect of souring the desire to achieve the goal because the work is just too much to get there and you lose site of the values with which you first started on your journey.

When your life journey gets you down, just stop for a moment and make sure you are still following your core values and beliefs. Especially make sure you are following <u>your</u> core values and beliefs and not someone else's. Then make the tiniest step forward possible. The smallest step towards your goal every day will give you a sense of achievement that builds exponentially the more you repeat it. Not taking any small step towards your goal each day quickly leads to depression.

TASK:

Think about something you want to achieve that is aligned with your core values and beliefs, but that has become difficult for you, or has dropped off your radar, or that you easily find excuses of 'no time' or other procrastinations for not taking action on.

Now think of the smallest step that you could take on this journey. It may be one phone call. It may be Google and research something. It might be making a short list of the reasons why you want to achieve that goal. It could be anything.

Now take that small step, and then tomorrow take another small step, and then the next day……….

LIVING

Corporate Culture

Suffrage and umbrance
Fear and pain
See the cloud
Stand in the rain

Stone cold hearts
Of modern beasts
The man in the suit
The bum in the street

Take no prisoners
Tell more lies
Corporate pleasure
Greed and pride

Board room battles
Stocks or bonds?
Give some more
Go way beyond

Family affairs
The hell is that?
Back to work
Caught in a trap

Sue the bastard
Sack the geek
You'll all obey
My insanity streak

Living

Rich and powerful
Are all but fleeting
But who the hell cares
Have I missed a meeting?

JR

Living
The First Step on the Journey....

Stocktake Time

And finally we come to Living and the completion of the foundation of our lives. Living is about having as many experiences as possible with the time you have. It's about being open to new ways of thinking and having a purpose that makes your life worth living.

Mind, Body, Soul and Living are the 4 Pillars that hold up the structure of our being. The purpose of your life is to live the best you can within the 4 Pillars. The stronger your pillars are the greater your life.

They all work in unison and are not mutually exclusive. If one is damaged then the whole structure becomes unstable and all work needs to focus on the damaged pillar.

It's all about balance. The balance between the 4 Pillars of Life.

So the first step in the journey of living is to take stock of where you are at. As we did back in the first step on Mind, you have to know where you are, and understand from what base you are launching your life.

What activities do you really enjoy?

When was the last time you decided to learn something new?

When was the last time you were spontaneous?

What experiences or goals do you have that you really want to have or achieve?

Don't think because you haven't seen the Eiffel Tower or been able to achieve a Black Belt in a Martial Art that you have failed. Don't look for big answers to the questions above. Remember it's not about the thing, it's about emotions. When you answer these questions think of the emotion that an experience gave you, that's what is important.

The last activity you enjoyed may have been hiking a track near your local town and being part of nature.

The last thing you may have decided to learn new was reading a book about self-defence.

The last time you were spontaneous may have been a weekend camping trip.

If even the smallest thing made you feel a sense of freedom or joy, even for a very short period, then that is what we are looking for. I'll repeat myself for about the 50th time in this book (but I don't care because it is that important), it's not the tangible material gains that are what makes your life have purpose, it's the emotions those tangible material gains give you.

De-Clutter

The point of a stock-take in a retail shop is to look at what stock you have left in the shop and understand what brands have sold well and what are not selling, and then to make adjustments and remove the poor performers and replace them with new and better options.

It's exactly the same with a life stock-take. We have a look at all the elements of our life. We look at what's working and what's not working. We decide if the things that aren't working should be kept and modified, or if we should get rid of them completely and replace them with something new and better. We also look closely at the things that are working. Just because something is working does not mean it is the right thing for us. You might be a high performer in your field of employment, respected by all, and making enormous amounts of money…………..but it's slowly killing you emotionally and physically. 'If it ain't broke don't fix it' is a metaphor for mediocrity.

The key to a meaningful de-clutter of your life is *'if in doubt, throw it out'*.
Emotions – anger, resentment, jealousy, depression

Behaviours – aggressiveness, the need to defend my opinions, selfishness

Surroundings – Negative people, negative news, acquaintances

Goals – Things that were important once but are now only being held onto for sentiment

> *'If it ain't broke don't fix it' is a metaphor for mediocrity.*
>
> JR

Every area and facet of your life should be examined, these are just a few examples above.

A Physical de-clutter is also an important process to undertake. Over the years we accumulate possessions and tangible things that we hold onto because we see them as part of who we are. All these things do is remind you of the person you used to be and not the person you want to be. Many people take comfort in these accumulated possessions because it gives them comfort and by always looking back they don't have to look forward and face the changes that may be ahead.

Stocktake Time

Get rid of anything that is of no use to you anymore, emotions, behaviours, people, and possessions. The less you have in your life, the more room there is for new experiences.

Living
The Second Step on the Journey....

Comfort Zone

Comfort Zones are like Black Holes. You don't have to try to stay in orbit around the comfort zone as the gravity of comfort does all the work for you. But one day you realise that you are drifting closer and closer to the centre, the Event Horizon, and all you can see ahead of you is darkness, so you decide to get out of the comfort zone orbit. Unfortunately you've been in the comfort zone too long and the gravity of comfort is too strong for you to get out, so all you can do now is wait to die.

Sounds a bit dramatic I know, but this happens to the majority of people day in day out. Most people don't realise until it's too late and then they are filled with regret and sadness at not having lived the life they really wanted. Their only option is to look for excuses, for someone to blame, as to why they haven't done the things they wanted. It's always someone else's fault never their own.

When I was in my mid-twenties I attended a training session on time management through my employer. It was a regular training day but there was one thing I took away from the day that really started the change in my thinking. Whilst it's never one individual thing that changes a person's life (unlike the movies where one amazing moment completely changes a person's life and they go from pathetic to amazing overnight), if I had to pinpoint a moment when a small spark was ignited in me, I would say it was then.

Comfort Zone

The trainer put 6 words up on the screen and said these were the antithesis of time management, personal development, and living a great life.

If……

But….

Maybe…..

Could've……

Would've……

Should've….

It really struck me that this was the way I was living my life.

If only all these things I can't control just fell into place for a change.

I'd love to do some things but it never works out for me.

I'll commit to that…maybe.

I could've done that if I really wanted to.

It would've been great if those people didn't stop me.

I should've got that promotion not him.

I was stuck in a comfort zone and looking for excuses and people or events to blame to justify why I wasn't reaching my potential. I was completely unaccepting of the things I couldn't control and just saw them as obstacles that stopped me even trying. I didn't want to try because I just kept getting disappointed.

I thought about these 6 words over the next few weeks and how relevant they were to my life. I started to see the story I was telling myself. The funny thing was that whilst I didn't want to get out of my comfort zone, I actually hated my comfort zone, but I was willing to accept a poor quality of life without even trying because I had convinced myself all the uncontrollable elements in the world where conspired against me.

Like I said, no one has one golden moment that changes their life forever, this is a fantasy that is promoted by many in the personal development industry to pander to the quick fix, impatient, and I want it all now, attitude of modern society. It simply doesn't work that way. But what does happen is moments of 'Satori', moments when for even a few seconds you see clearly, you have a 'light-bulb' moment. These small moments of Satori build on each other over time and start to drive your life out of the comfort zone.

Your Comfort Zone is Shrinking

Using the cosmology analogy again, unlike the universe which is continuously expanding, without intervention your comfort zone will constantly get smaller the older you get. You know the people, the cranky old Aunty who whinges about everything, the guy who leaves his home only to go to the pub and complains that society has him trapped.

Our comfort zones tend to expand from birth to when we finish school and start work. It's at that point when control of our comfort zone falls onto us as individuals. Our comforts zones expand through childhood as we look at the world without judgement and we try everything we can without fear of failure or reproach. But when we get into the workforce, the 'real world', and we start to run up against a vastly more complex environment than when we were children, we often start to feel lost and out of control. At times like this we will fall back into the familiar, back into the roles we know. As I said earlier comfort zones are not necessarily nice places, they are often places we hate to be, but the point is we know what the out-

> *People always tell you to think outside the box.....I still feel like I'm just trying to find the little sticker on the box that says 'This way up'.*
>
> *JR*

comes will be from the actions we take in our comfort zone. Even if the outcomes are bad it is not a surprise for us, and that points to the core of a comfort zone.....the fear of the unknown.

If we don't live consciously and remain unaware of our actions and automatic thoughts, we will continue in our comfort zone, and as we get older there are less and less things we like to change, and as such something you may have been happy to do last year, is now outside the comfort zone because you are uncertain of the outcome or you just don't like the fact it has changed.

TASK:

The older we get the smaller our comfort zone gets and it's critical we keep pushing the boundaries. Take a moment to consider your comfort zone. Look at every aspect of your life including but not limited to your health and fitness, career, financial, relationships, adventure etc.

Now think about the things you want to achieve that are outside your comfort zone. What story are you telling yourself as to why you can't achieve those goals? Why are they outside the circle? Your goal should be to expand your circle to encompass those things. Expansion of our comfort zone is the aim in life.

Living
The Third Step on the Journey....

A Sense of Adventure

You know what the difference between an Old Boy and an Old Man is? It has nothing to do with age. You can be an Old Man at 30 and an Old Boy at 80. It has everything to do with your sense of adventure.

It's nothing new, the adage that it's not your age but your state of mind that counts, but like so many things with our own personal development, we say the words but we take no action. We think like Tarzan but we live like Jane.

A sense of adventure is what keeps us young, it's what motivates us to get up in the morning, it's what we find passion in. It is not about climbing Mt Everest, or jumping out of a plane at 10,000 feet. It can be those things but the definition of what having a Sense of Adventure means is critical to understanding how it applies in our lives. If it were just the big ticket items like Everest or Sky Diving then only 1% of us would bother and the rest would sit on the couch, watch TV and moan about how boring our lives are.

> *An Old Man thinks like Tarzan but lives like Jane.*
>
> **JR**

So what is having a sense of adventure all about?

First and foremost it is about having an open mind and being open to new experiences without any preconceived ideas or judgements. What stops most people having a sense of adventure is the judgements they make about other people and experiences they are not used to. I go back to our Comfort Zone discussion, when something is outside our comfort zone we will subconsciously look for excuses as to why we can't do that, or look for someone to blame when we don't even try.

The word Adventure could easily be replaced with Curiosity. Adventure tends to invoke the big bold and brave things whereas Curiosity is simply about having more experiences, and that is what a Sense of Adventure is, having as many experiences in your life as you can, big, small and in between.

My Old Boys Thai Boxing club (OBTB) is a great example of having a sense of adventure. The OBTB clubs are all about learning fight skills and putting them into practice through pad work and sparring, in an environment that is encouraging and pushes you out of your comfort zone. 90% of the Old Boys who come and try it have never thrown a punch in anger in their entire lives, and without an environment with likeminded individuals, would never enter a normal Boxing Gym or Muay Thai Stable.

It's important to understand where the adventure starts. It doesn't start once you've climbed Everest, or completed that goal you set yourself. Like every aspect of life, Adventure is in the emotion of the Journey, not the destination. It's an adventure in itself when an Old Boy makes the decision to go to an OBTB class and learn some fight skills. That decision has immediately taken him outside his comfort zone and that is the adventure right there.

The smallest things in life can be adventurous. Deciding to learn another language is an adventure, it's something that is different from who you think you are as a person. Adventure

> *The adventure starts when you make the decision to take the first step.*
>
> *JR*

is the continual questioning of who you believe you are, or who you think other people believe you are. Never settle for the same old same old. Keep challenging yourself and you'll be amazed at what this continual search for adventure does to your emotions and your well-being. By being constantly focused on your life as one big adventure is exciting and can be a life's purpose in and of itself.

TASK:

Every day for the next week I want you to do something completely different to your normal routine, do something totally out of the ordinary. Do something that people who know you every day would not believe you did. But don't tell them. The point is you are seeking an adventurous life for you and your own emotions. If your motive for seeking an adventurous life is to have people tell you how amazing you are, then you are completely on the wrong track. All you are doing then is making the happiness in your life contingent on what other people say….and that is a recipe for anxiety and depression because in the end it doesn't matter what you do, you can't control the thoughts and reactions of other people.

Living
The Fourth Step on the Journey....

Zen Living

Zen living is a way of managing your mind, attitude and behaviours that is more pertinent now in modern society than ever before in history. As we become more and more connected as a society, as the 24/7 flood of information threatens to overwhelm our thinking and turn us into information zombies, the way of Zen Living offers a solution and a way to combat 'connection fatigue'.

'Connection fatigue' is the term I give to the 24/7 connectedness of the world. We wake up in the morning and the first thing we do is check Facebook. The last thing we do before we go to bed is surf the internet. All through the day we receive emails, texts, Facebook notifications, and news. Denzel Washington, the Hollywood actor, made a great statement once when asked by a reporter what he made of the media and the issue of 'too much news'. He responded –

"If you don't read the news your uninformed, if you read the news you're misinformed. It's not about the truth anymore, it's about being first".

As humans we can only absorb a certain amount of information at any one time. Now our brains are the most sophisticated computer on earth, but what makes it so sophisticated is that it can take in every bit of information delivered through the 5 senses, but it subconsciously chooses what to focus on and retain, and the way it does this is through our experiences. What has shaped our thinking during our lifetime, what

> *"If you don't read the news your uninformed, if you read the news you're misinformed. It's not about the truth anymore, it's about being first".*
>
> **Denzel Washington**

influences, both nature and nurture, have created the person we perceive ourselves to be. Through all those experiences our brain will then choose what it deems to be the most important to you as a person and to your survival.

The media understand this phenomena and as our world has become more and more connected, with more and more information, it has become a race to be both first with information and also to pander to what people's automatic thoughts will perceive as important for their survival as a person. Don't be flippant and dismiss this, it's a base fact of human existence and the media and the marketing world know it. So more and more the need to be first has overcome the responsibility to be right, to investigate and get to the real truth of matters. Be careful what you believe, investigate everything for yourself, and investigate with facts not what others tell you.

Zen

Zen is a school of Buddhism originally formed in China but it really developed its strengths in Japanese cultural history. Zen is really about understanding what it means to have a 'Buddha-nature', and then taking action and living that way.

Whilst having a 'Buddha-nature' is a detailed study on its own, I would refer you to **SOUL The Sixth Step on the Journey – Warrior Code**. Living the Code of the Warrior in everyday life is the essence of what Zen Living means. Becoming conscious of the way you think, react, and behave in simple everyday situations, and changing your behaviour to be a better person.

Living in the Moment

Zen living is about living in the moment as much as possible. Focusing on what is in front of us right now. Many people who are sceptical of this approach say that living in the present is burying your head in the sand. In fact it is the exact opposite, the people who focus on the past or the future are not prepared to face up to the actual real world in the moment and are either looking for excuses from their past for why things are the way they are now, or hoping something magical will happen in the future to change things.

When you focus on the past all you do is regret. When you focus on the future all you do is worry. This does not mean you ignore the past or the future…….but I just told you to forget about them and focus on the present didn't I? This is the key to understanding Zen living.

The Past

We must learn from the past. If we don't assess how we performed in the past how will we ever be able to make the changes we need in the present? If you keep doing what you've always done, you'll continue to get what you've always got. The key word is REGRET. Stop looking back and thinking 'I should have done this' or 'I was stupid'. Whatever has happened in the past, you acted at that time based on your automatic thoughts and conditioning at that time. Of course it's easy to look back and say I should've done something different, but it is what it is, you can't change it, and so learn from it so you can change the way you act in the future. This is conscious living. Playing the blame game is not learning.

> *The past is what it is. Learn from it and let it go.*
>
> *JR*

By looking back and finding an excuse for your behaviour is pandering to your own ego. Your attitude is the only thing in life you have 100% control over and until you understand that and accept that, you will continue to look back with regret, and will be destined to make the same mistakes over and over.

The Future

The future is unknown. The future is the analogy of planting seeds. It depends what seed you plant now as to what crop you will yield in the future. What makes you think that worrying in the present, about what will happen in the future, will yield you happiness and no further worry? It's ridiculous but it's the way we are programmed. But remember the future never comes, there is never a time when there is no future and planting the seeds of worry in the present means you will reap worry in the future.

All you can do in the present is influence the future by changing your attitude to how you view what happens to you in the present. There is no other answer, yet whilst it sounds simple it is difficult as it goes against the grain of what our brains are programmed by society to do, but the effort to master this process is worth more than anything you can imagine.

Live the Zen

So……study your past without regret, regardless of what has happened. Understand ways you can change your attitude to the things that happened to you and apply those changes in the present.

> *The Future is built in the Now.*
>
> *JR*

Plan for the future. Have goals and targets to achieve them. Break those steps down into smaller and smaller achievable steps, then act on those steps in the present moment without worry about how those steps will work out. You can look back and review the success or otherwise of these steps later, and make adjustments.

Don't regret the past and don't worry about the future. Study your past and make changes to your attitude in the present that will influence the future. Then rinse and repeat……

TASK:

Go into your past and pick one moment or one action that you regret. Think about why you regret that action. It's not the action itself that you regret, it's the emotional impact it had on you then and has on you now. You may have upset a close friend, or done something that hurt others.

Now put yourself back in that situation but with the maturity you have now. How would you like to have acted or how would you act now? What changes did you make to your attitude? How did you change your emotions at that time?

Now take that different attitude you have applied and think of a situation in the present where you know you could apply that attitude and get a better outcome. Run the scenario through your brain like a day dream. Feel the emotions. What emotion is throwing you off track? It may simply be that you just hate the person in front of you, which is fine, then you know you have to let go of the things that have caused you to dislike that person. Remember you are not doing any of this for the other person, it's all about you. They will continue to be an asshole I'm sure, but you can't change that so stop getting angry about it.

Now think about a specific thing you worry about into the future. Often its financial worries, or family, it could be anything. Remember that you have no control over the actual outcome, the only control you have is over your attitude and the actions you take in the present. Come up with 1 attitude trait you can change right now in your life that will influence a different outcome in the future. It may be more tolerance for a person, it may be making an effort to become conscious of your anger when it arises.

Now think of 1 action you can take now that will influence the future. It may be taking a time management course, it may be as simple as making a phone call to someone you have been avoiding.

Overall keep it simple, don't try and get too complex with your past analysis, or with changing too many things in your attitude at one time. That just leads to frustration and worry…… the reverse of what you are trying to achieve. Just take small steps…….there is no rush.

Living
The Fifth Step on the Journey....

The Intangibles

This is a recurring theme as it applies to each of the 4 Pillars of Life and is a critical element in changing your life. It's the Intangible, not the tangible, which gives meaning and purpose to life.

It's so important to clearly understand this statement as it is the root of true happiness. But what is true happiness? This is where most people's search for meaning, purpose and happiness tends to get lost in translation. Firstly it's important to understand the difference between long term happiness and short term pleasure. Short term pleasure is the feelings of joy you get when you achieve a goal, buy that car, see a really funny movie, or get drunk. You are happy in the moment. Of course being in the moment is one of our key goals, but being in the moment without sowing the seeds for future happiness, is simply sweeping the problems under the carpet. Modern society has become expert at masking the unhappiness and lack of purpose in our lives through the possession of tangible things. Marketing panders to these traits all the time. Marketing aims to associate a product with something that you think will make you happy. It's not the tangible product that companies are selling, it's the intangible emotion that product will give you that they are trying to convince you of.

This has been a recurring theme through this journey, and for good reason. I want to drum into you how important it is to understand that it is your emotions and feelings that make true happiness, not short term pleasure or tangible possessions.

True happiness that comes from the intangible emotions and feelings that are produced by the experiences that you have every day, is where you will find yourself at peace.

TASK:

In a discussion about intangibles, when you're asked to focus on what makes you happy, it's difficult not to think about the tangibles because that's how we are programmed. But…..

Think back in your life to a time you were truly happy and you felt at peace with yourself and the world around you. Many of you will immediately say there has never been a time….. but you are constricted by your current thoughts and you are simply not moving out of the world around you now. Go back to your childhood, it doesn't matter if you were 5 or 50. Or the feeling lasted 1 minute or 1 week, it's the moment we want to identify.

Think about what that moment entailed. What was the situation at the time? What was happening around you? What feelings did you have? What emotions were creating this sense of happiness?

For me I know music often is a time I truly feel happy, both listening and playing. It's a time when I feel at peace and in the moment.

For others it could be playing sport, or reading, or being in nature. It's not the thing or the place that's important, it's the emotions that are generated.

This exercise is harder than it looks but just relax and take some time alone to work through this exercise. You will begin to notice that every instance in your life that produced strong feelings of peace and happiness was the product of how you felt about and perceived the tangible situation or object in front of you.

Living
The Sixth Step on the Journey....

Stop Waiting for the Right Time

You've heard it a million times, there is never a right time, but procrastination is such a part of who we are that we can successfully argue to ourselves that it's not procrastination it's that we can't start because of this thing or that situation.

STOP!! You're procrastinating.

The biggest reason people have for procrastinating is they focus on the end goal and not the next step. In writing this book there is no way I would have even started if I looked at the end goal of a 78,000 word book, that is just too much to think of and is unachievable, but my goal was 250 words per day every day. That's all. 250 words per day would seem like a poor effort for an accomplished writer, but I am not an accomplished writer, I was average at best at school English (once I was even accused of it being my second language) and I had

> *A rough plan started today, is better than a perfect plan started tomorrow.*

never attempted anything like this before. So 250 words for me was what I could achieve without burning out. I set a goal based on 250 words per day which equated to 300 days writing, and then I forgot about the end goal and just did my bit every day. I just started and only focused on the next step.

In writing this book the goal posts have also shifted. The focus changed slightly as I began to realise certain things during the writing process. I changed the way I was doing things and how

I was focusing the script. I could never have envisaged these changes, which have all been for the better, before I started, they only came to light because I made a start, and that is the key to accomplishing anything......Just make a start.

Your plan will never be perfect, and waiting until a plan is perfect before you start will never happen, there will always be some risks that you can't mitigate and in fact there will be many more things you don't even realise, that will raise their heads after you've started that you never would have identified beforehand. But this is all about the adventure of the journey (Remember our discussion in **LIVING –The Third Step on the Journey - A Sense of Adventure?**).

The secret is to build momentum and you build momentum by taking the smallest step possible the first time and then building on that. When you take off in a car you don't take off in 4th gear, if you do the engine will become overwhelmed and stall. You take off in 1st gear at the slowest speed and then build up momentum. It's exactly the same with achieving anything in life. Don't focus on going 100 miles an hour, just start moving.

Also stop thinking you don't have the resources or you don't have the required skill. I have no skill in writing, I've never attempted anything like this before and I know it's no masterpiece, but it's something I wanted to do, I felt I had something to say, and so I started without any skill or knowledge about what I was doing.

Do what you can, with what you have, where you are, learn, adapt, and enjoy the adventure.

Do what you can now, with what you have now, where you are now, learn, adapt, and enjoy the adventure.

TASK:

Go back to **MIND – Step 3 of the Journey – Identifying Goals**. Pick one of your goals and identify one single action you can do today (not tomorrow) that will be a step towards this goal. Keep the action small. It may be a phone call, or google research a topic, but whatever it is keep it small and do it. Then tomorrow I want you to do the same thing. Every day for the next 30 days, pick a small action and make it happen. I don't care what else is happening in your life, the smallest task can always be achieved if you really want it.

Living
The Seventh Step on the Journey....

Travel Time

A common theme with many people is the desire to travel and see and experience different places, but the tradition of our society has always been, get a good job, work hard, save your money, then when you retire you can do all the things you've ever wanted to do.

I could not disagree more strongly with this philosophy and the reason I do is because of my own father. My father worked hard his whole life, both on the land and in a government position. He saved his money and was frugal in all aspects of his life. He had a goal to buy a campervan when he retired and travel around Australia and see all the remote areas of this wonderful country. Well he worked hard saved his money, retired, and then died of prostate cancer without ever even buying a campervan.

He wanted to have all these experiences but was always too busy and he couldn't afford the time off work, but he retired with several months of accumulated leave plus 6 months of long service leave not used. In the end there was always an excuse why he couldn't do it. He was brought up in a society that frowned on any sort of luxury like travel, and if he was to take 3 months off and go travelling it would have been so far outside his comfort zone that he just couldn't bring himself to do it.

I understand that time away from work and the cost of travelling and creating experiences can seem to be prohibitive, but stop thinking that travel and experience has to be travelling all over Europe for a month at a time. I took my first trip overseas to Italy when I was 41 years old. Prior to that with a growing family and career I couldn't afford an overseas trip, but you know what we had done every year for the last 20? We had made one small trip every year, my wife and my 3 girls, like driving 4 hours from our home to Cairns and visiting the rainforest for a week. Going camping for a few days at a nice creek. Flying to Sydney for a week. I can tell you with passion that the memories we have created as a family through these small trips is incredible. The simple experiences of being together, and the little things that have happened along the way that have made us all laugh, and that still make us laugh today, are the Intangibles that I spoke about in **LIVING The Fifth Step on the Journey**.

The point of what I am saying is you have to get out of your little bubble. The world doesn't end at the outskirts of your suburb. Get out there and broaden your experiences, see places you've always wanted to see and create memories that you and your family can enjoy together forever. Do it now……….who is to say you won't be dead when you wake up in the morning?

TASK:

Simple…….Pick an experience you want to have that involves travelling to somewhere you have not been. Work out how you are going to do it and when. Lock it in and start experiencing!!

Living
The Eight Step on the Journey....

Work, Career, Passion

We spend 40% to 50% of our waking hours at work during our lifetime. We then spend a majority of the balance waking hours either worrying about work or dreading work, in any event it is always top of our minds and is the greatest influence on our lives.

So many personal development books talk about finding your passion and then just go out and do it. Unfortunately that is an unrealistic load of bollocks that feeds on people's false hopes and dreams. Sounds a bit harsh I know but let's be realistic. For the majority of us we won't have the opportunity to make a hobby or a sport, or a passion, our primary source of income, but that does not mean we should be satisfied with a dead end job that would suck the colour out of a rainbow it's that depressing.

In my analysis of this major component of our lives I break it down into 3 separate categories –

1. Work
2. Career
3. Passion

Work

We all work but this definition is doing something that you may not like and is not where you want to be or what you want to do for the rest of your life, but is what you have to do now to get by. We tend to start 'work' early in our lives and then progress through to a career but the Global Financial Crisis (GFC) of 2008 created a whole new set of rules especially for men who thought they were well into their career only to find it disappear from their grasp and having to turn back to 'work'.

Because work is something you do for the money and is not necessarily your career goal it can be uninspiring and very tedious or stressful. When you are forced to work there are two areas I see as important –

1. Keep your career goal alive. Don't lose sight of where you want to be. No matter how distant or impossible that goal may be, keep it alive and keep taking small steps towards it.

2. Don't despise where you are but also don't accept your current status. Strive for more.

You don't have to enjoy what you do, you just need to enjoy how you do it. As I said above, don't let yourself get to the point you despise what you are doing. See it as necessary now but a stepping stone to a better future, but while you have to work you need to change the only thing you can control, and that is your attitude. It doesn't matter what you are doing, you can at least enjoy the way you do it. The way to do that is to be mindful in every minute. Stop thinking about the past or the future and stop being angry about where you are at, bring your complete focus to what you are doing, and be completely absorbed in the moment. You're a delivery driver,

> *You don't have to enjoy what you do, you just need to enjoy how you do it. JR*

operating a grader, working in an office it doesn't matter. Do what you are doing the best you can do it. Be the best delivery driver possible, be the best grader driver possible, be the best manager possible. This combined with keeping your career goal alive is a means to staying sane in an insane workplace.

Career

Your career is what you have studied for, what you have trained for, what you achieve all the relevant tickets and qualifications for. It's what you know how to do and what you see yourself as doing for the greater part of your working life.

At this stage, unlike work, you have a genuine interest in what you are doing and that often comes with a goal and desire to be more and more successful. But be careful about where you focus. If you focus solely on climbing the corporate ladder or getting that management role, you run the risk of losing focus on being the best at what you do every day. There are so many things including other people's actions and a multitude of other influences that can intercede into your goal to climb the ladder and you run the risk of becoming stressed and losing momentum when things don't go your way. A career can easily become work if you stop focusing on being the best you can be and start focusing on things you can't control.

Passion

Passion is a difficult thing to come by. Less than 1% of people have what can be defined as a true passion that they can make a career out of. The majority have differing levels of interest in different things. Passion is a strong word and for most people when they are asked to state what they are passionate about, they really feel a bit lost and perhaps a bit inadequate because they don't have a passion. Don't feel bad, everyone is the same. Stop thinking that you need to be madly in love with something and that's all you think about doing for it to be a passion. Start to look at simple things that you enjoy or hobbies that you enjoy wasting time on. Playing my guitar is something I enjoy doing and enjoy wasting some time on. I'm never going to make a living out of it (unless low skill and bad singing ever become a thing…) but it's something I enjoy doing in my hours outside the office that eats into that time we would normally spend mindlessly in front of the TV or social media.

Having said all that think about some of the things you enjoy doing and don't limit yourself on where they may take you. As you know I have been a martial artist for many years and I started an 'Old Boys Thai Boxing' club back in 2009 just for a bit of training with some guys who were as slow as I was. That club has grown to become something that runs 4 days a week and is a real passion. I make no money out of it but I get so much enjoyment from it, and the experiences I have had there have lead me to write this book. If you told me when I was 25 I would run a martial arts club and write a book I would have laughed at you. Don't ever limit your thinking about where a passion can take you.

> *Don't ever limit your thinking about where a passion can take you.*
>
> *JR*

Future Certainty

If there is one thing we need to get used to, it's that there is no certainty in career anymore. The world is changing so rapidly that careers are becoming extinct at a rapid rate and new careers are opening up all the time. Technology is creating exponentially rapid change and some people who thought 10 years ago this is what they would do for life, will find themselves in 10 years wondering where their job went.

I was born in 1969 and I feel my era is a little unique. When I was in high school I saw the very first computers introduced. I was about 16 I think and the computers were the big box with the green writing on the screen and the large floppy disk that could hold about 128b of information……but it's all relevant. At that time it was amazing and there were only 10 computers for 400 students.

When I started work there were no mobile phones or email and there was only 1 computer for the whole office. By 1995 I had my first mobile, but with no ability to text, and email still hadn't arrived. By 1998 we had Blackberry's and access to email and life changed because you couldn't escape work. You were on call 24/7. By 2000 we all had Laptops and things really started to heat up.

I believe my era is unique in that we were born before this modern technology and experienced life without the constant 24/7 connection to the world, but we've had to adapt and change and make all the mistakes along the way. It doesn't make us any better it just means we've had a unique insight into both sides of the technological fence. (Thankfully we did most of our stupid stuff before there was Facebook evidence…..)

What it all means though is that the days when you got a job or trade and that was what you would do for the rest of your life, are gone. There is no loyalty in big business it's purely a numbers game. If the profits aren't there then there are no jobs. Don't bury your head in the sand on this issue or look to lay blame, your livelihood depends on it. Keep yourself informed, read, research, and keep up with technology as best as you can. It's critical to your future that you are able to adapt and change to meet current demands and needs.

TASK:

Do you **Work**? What do you really want to do? Do you have a plan to get there? Are you taking action everyday towards that goal, or are you finding all the excuses and people to blame as possible?

Where are you at in your **Career**? Are you moving towards your ultimate goal? Are you focused on being the best you can possible be at what you do every day, or have you lost this focus? Think hard about what you do. How will it be impacted by future technology? Get online and research this. Be very specific about the impacts on what you do in 5 years, 10 years, 20 years. Put a plan in place to train and adapt to meet the coming changes.

Do you have a **Passion**? What do you enjoy doing? Are you engaging in this activity enough? What's stopping you? What reasons do you tell yourself you can't do that thing you enjoy? Be realistic and don't just blame time or money, they are the superficial excuses that you use to mask the real reasons. Often the real reasons have more to do with what you think other people will think, than anything else.

Living
The Ninth Step on the Journey....

Time Management

If there is one key element to your work and life balance that you should adopt it's a good Time Management strategy. Now there are thousands of books and blogs and YouTube tutorials on Time Management and none of them are right, nor are any of them wrong. The Time Management strategy you choose needs to be closely linked to the type of person you are. It needs to reflect your nature and attributes. There is no one size fits all and you should experiment with as many strategies as you can research and find what works for you.

Everyone is different. Some people are methodical and detailed, others think outside the box and are creative. A methodical list based time management strategy will not work for a creative type, and a high level prompt based system will not work for the methodical type. So you need to experiment with different methods. You will likely find that there is no one particular system that works for you but that you will end up developing your own system that is a mash-up of various types and styles.

> *A Time Management strategy is inexorably linked to your personal behavioural traits. Find out what type of person you are first, then find a time management strategy that suits you. One size does not fit all.*
>
> **JR**

One thing that remains consistent though between all systems is being able to define the following parameters in terms of your life and its priorities –

1. Importance
2. Urgency

Beware there are two very big pitfalls in Time Management and they both revolve around the definition of Important and Urgent. As I've said throughout this book the 24/7 world of information we live in is breeding a 'need to be first' mentality.

As an individual you can very easily fall into the trap of whatever is in front of you is important and urgent.

As an employee you have a doubled edged sword as your boss can easily fall into the same trap except he is delegating his 'need to be first' down to you.

Importance

When we talk Time Management everyone thinks about their work or their job, the day to day things they have to do. We come at time management from a negative perspective, 'what do I <u>HAVE</u> to do today'?

Firstly time management is about managing all the time you have available to you. By limiting it to just managing all those things you hate but have to do at work you are missing out on an incredibly valuable tool that if instituted into your life proper can reap enormous rewards down the track.

This is why I suggest there are two time management programs running in your life. The main one deals with your whole life and all the things that you have identified within the 4 Pillars that represent your values and core beliefs. One sub-component of this strategy is a single heading called work/career and under that then is a separate time management strategy dealing with those elements specifically that will help you get through your work day and be the best you can be at your job.

The key here is to change your focus. Why do we only think that what we do in our day to day job deserves time management? Because at work we are accountable to a boss, outside we are only accountable to ourselves and it's easy to tell ourselves we are too busy or too tired or too lazy. Why are we the worst boss in the world when it comes to our own life?

Start changing your definition of important and put yourself first. This does not mean then your job is let go, what it means is you compartmentalise your life. You have to be at work for 40 or 50 hours a week so make those hours productive being the best you can be, but then the other 50% of your waking time is your life, so get cracking on what's important to you and start living a life.

> *Be the Boss of your own life.*
>
> *JR*

Urgency

The need to be first analogy used by Denzel Washington as we discussed earlier in this book, is a cancer that eats away at what's important and kills our goals and ambitions, because we are constantly distracted by what needs to be done now rather than what is important to us.

Urgent can be difficult when you are an employee because you are not just living your definition of Important and Urgent but you are living your boss's as well. I have a solution for that……..get over it, that's life and the majority of people in the world have to deal with that on a day to day basis. You can't control them. BUT…..without a time management tool as part of your arsenal you will certainly make it as hard as possible for yourself.

My System

My system of Time Management is a hybrid of various methodologies I have researched, studied or been taught over the years. The Matrix that I reflect below is not my invention and is something I was taught on a training session when I was in my early 20's and it has served me very well in my work, my career and in my personal development goals.

The key to the matrix is not just having a clear comprehension of what is Important and what is Urgent to you, but also the relationship between the two. What is important is not always urgent, and what is urgent is not always important.

	Urgent	Not Urgent
Important	1	2
Not Important	3	4

In my **Personal Life Goals** system everything falls into 4 categories as above –

- Category 1 – Is both Important and Urgent
- Category 2 – is Important but not Urgent

- Category 3 – is NOT Important but Urgent
- Category 4 – is NOT Important and NOT Urgent

At all times you should be working in Categories 1 and 2. If you have assessed your Importance and Urgency properly to meet your personal agenda, then anything in Category 3 and 4 mean only one thing –

YOU'RE WASTING TIME!

However be very careful when you are assessing what is important and what is urgent. It is very easy to just say everything is important and everything is urgent. It takes a clear focus on your goals and your values and core beliefs and a strict ability to cull what does not meet that criteria. When it comes to importance if the task in front of you does not assist you in taking a step towards your core goals or your core values, then why are you even entertaining it? Probably because some else said it was important. **Be very clear on this. If you do not get your assessment of what is important in line with who you want to be, then time management is useless.**

Once you have sorted what is important and what is not, then comes the assessment of what is urgent. I assess Urgent as 'if I don't do this today it will have major implications for my goals tomorrow'. In other words if it absolutely does not need to be done today then it is not urgent.

Time Management is a skill not just a formula you follow. The core of the success of Time Management strategies is in the alignment of what is Important and what is Urgent, with your personal goals and values. Put a strategy in place and keep modifying.

In the sub-category of the **<u>Work System</u>** I work within 8 categories. The 4 main categories above of Importance and Urgency still apply but I have an additional 4 that are specific to my business. I run a Project Management business in the property development industry and as the sole owner manager of my business I need to look at all aspects of my business and as such I firstly break my work down into the following 4 categories –

1. Prospective new work
2. Existing Client Tasks
3. Marketing
4. Administration

You should assess what categories work best within your job. It doesn't have to be limited to 4 and can be any topic that is relevant. Note that I prioritise these actions with prospective new work or clients taking the priority, closely followed by existing jobs and clients, then marketing and then administration.

So how does all this work?

At the end of each day I gather together all the outstanding tasks, emails, phone messages, and anything else, and I sort them into the 4 categories as listed above.

I then take the first category (Prospective New Work) and I sort those tasks into important or Not Important. I do this for all of the 4 categories.

I then take the first pile (Prospective New Work – Important) and sort that pile into Urgent or Not Urgent.

I repeat this process for all the categories.

It sounds like a lot of work but this process takes me less than 5 minutes at the end of each day and the time it saves me, and the stress it removes is absolutely invaluable to the success of my business and my ability to deliver on time and on budget for my clients and to keep my business fresh and at the forefront of the industry.

I strongly recommend putting your Time Management strategy in place at the end of each day rather than first up at the start of the day. The reason is two-fold –

1. It allows you to leave your work behind and helps you destress at night knowing you have a plan ready for the next day.

2. It allows you to attack the most important tasks the second you start work in the morning, when you are fresh and ready to go. No time wasted.

At the end of this sorting process I have 8 folders, numbered in priority from 1-8 as follows –

1. Prospective New Work – Urgent

2. Existing Client Tasks – Urgent

3. Marketing – Urgent

4. Administration – Urgent

5. Prospective New Work – Not Urgent

6. Existing Client Tasks – Not Urgent

7. Marketing – Not Urgent

8. Administration – Not Urgent

Each new day I then work my way through each folder in order of priority from 1-8. What this does for me is that when you have those days where you get interrupted and you just can't achieve all that you wanted to that day, by starting at priority 1 at least I know I have taken action on the thing that is most important to my future that day. If I get through the items in folders 1-4 and I don't get to 5-8 then that is a good day, I just resort the balance folders again at the end of the day.

> *Time Management should be applied to your whole life, not just your working day.*
>
> *JR*

Note that there is no reference to Important in the above 8 categories. If you weeded out something that was Not Important in the sorting phase then that should either be thrown in the bin, or delegated (as long as you're then not wasting that other persons time with something that is truly unimportant).

In summary Time Management should be applied to your whole life not just your job. Be very clear on what is Important and what is Urgent, then combine the two to create meaningful outcomes. Research and learn as many Time Management Strategies as possible and work out what works best for your style of job and your style of personality. Then make it your own by altering and changing to suit your own circumstances.

Living
The Tenth Step on the Journey....

Status Anxiety

Few things dominate our world and our individual lives like the need for Status. The great modern day Philosopher Alain De Botton has spent a lifetime analysing this very issue (among his vast array of studies and topics) and has coined the term 'Status Anxiety'. He has written an excellent book on the subject.

What is Status Anxiety? In summary Status Anxiety is our deep seated, and often unconscious worries, about what others think of us; about whether we're judged a success or a failure, a winner or a loser. Most Old Boys will say 'I don't care what others think of me', but that in itself is a declaration that we do actually care. By saying to someone 'I don't care' is expressing our desire to have that person think of us as having it all together, of being someone who is strong and in control of his life.

Whilst we generally align Status with our financial situation, Alain De Botton's definition of Status Anxiety is significantly more far reaching than simple financial status, but the basis of the thinking and the outcomes remain the same.

One of the major issues facing the Old Boy generation is the constant media barrage of 'success stories'. A whole industry has grown up around the world of Financial Anxiety. Images of successful people who have made it big from a simple idea and wealthy or famous people being held up by the media as somehow superior to the sweaty masses.

Now I definitely don't mean to undermine success. I am genuinely happy for people who have made it, worked hard, taken risks and provided employment for people along the way. Without these people, money does not flow around the economy and the economy is like a river, when the flow dries up so does the life in, on, and surrounding the river.

I was told a story early in my career to explain in simplistic terms how the economy works and has always stuck with me. The Global Financial Crisis only served to enhance the relevance of this lesson. Some of you may have heard this story before in different formats, but this is my version –

A travelling salesman drives into a small country town late one afternoon. It's hot, he's tired, he misses his family and the day has not been a roaring success. He pulls into the first motel he sees. As a travelling salesman he knows motels and backwater hostels, and never judges a book by its cover, and tonight he really needs a nice bed and a good night's sleep.

He enters reception and an old lady is at the counter and greets him cheerfully. The salesman smiles and enquires on a room for the night. Yes they have several rooms available, it's been very quiet in this town since the mine closed down and business has been hard. The salesman smiles and asks to inspect the room first. The old lady seems to lose some of her welcoming spirit but agrees and asks the man to place a $50 deposit for the key. He agrees, hands over the $50 and goes out the door to inspect the room.

As soon as the salesman has rounded the corner the old lady locks the door, grabs the $50 and walks briskly across the street to the local newsagent. She is behind in her account with the newsagent for delivery of the morning papers for the motel, but *everyone is trying to look after everyone else in this small town. The newsagent is surprised and pleased with the $50 reduction in the account and thanks the old lady.*

Within seconds of the old lady leaving, the newsagent locks his front door, slips out the back and into the butcher next door. The newsagent owes the butcher $100 for last month's meat order and means to pay it off as soon as he can. The butcher is grateful and thanks the newsagent.

When the newsagent leaves the butcher quickly locks his front door and walks around the corner to a small house. He knocks and the door is opened by a beautiful middle aged lady who greets him with a smile. 'Maria' is the local prostitute and the butcher owes her $50 from last nights 'date'. She smiles thanks him and bids him come again.

'Maria' then immediately leaves her house and walks back around the corner and across the street and enters the reception of the motel. She is greeted by the old lady warmly and Maria pays the old Lady the $50 she owes her for the room rental for her 'date' with the butcher the night before.

Just then the salesman walks back in and says that unfortunately he is not satisfied with the standard of the room and he will not be taking the room for the night. He hands back the key and the old lady refunds his $50.......

On the surface it seems that no one has won, but this economy has just grown by $200!

Now I am no economist, and those educated amongst my readers will pick holes in the economics of this story, but it's not a story about economics, it's a story about financial attitude. There are two parts to the story of financial attitude –

1. How do you react to your circumstances
2. What influence do you have over your circumstances

How do you react to your financial circumstances?

Take your current financial situation, how do you view yourself? Are you successful? Are you a failure? Do you want more? Do you struggle? Do you try your hardest only to have 'The Man' always beat you to the punch?

What drives you financially? Is it material possessions? Is it responsibility to family? Is it the desire to travel? Is it the perception you want others to have of you? Is it the future lifestyle you desire?

Where do you want to be? If you're reading this book I'm assuming you don't have a burning desire to be a useless lazy bastard, but does that mean you want to be wealthy beyond imagination, or simply be financially independent? What is financial independence?

What's stopping you? Is it your upbringing? Is it your boss? Is it your education? Is it where you live? Is it others with more money than you?

There are so many questions that financial status throws up, because in our modern society, wealth and the ability to trade in commodities is driven by the basic human instinct of survival. Understand that we are animals, with a very strong fight or flight sense hard wired into our brains and nervous system. What else is anxiety other than the fear for my survival? Now you may say that I'm anxious about my work or my wife and these are non-life threatening issues, but look closer. It's true that in the modern era we don't face life threatening animals or situations at every turn, but what we face, rather what we are bombarded with in modern society, is a sense of Identity.

Writers such as Eckhart Tolle call this the Ego. It is a collection of experiences, both nature (our genetic predisposition) and nurture (the environment we were raised in), that create an intangible set of beliefs about who we are. Note I said intangible, this is not the tangible thing such as 'I am an engineer' or 'I am a labourer', but rather it is the intangible elements such as –

'I am impatient'

'I am always being taken advantage of'

'I have always been unlucky'

'People with money always win and are untrustworthy'

But this is not all negative. It also includes things such as –

'I am a very good athlete'

'I am the best engineer this firm has'

'I am a better father than my father ever was'

It is worth the exercise to sit quietly with pen and paper (and I find a Red Wine helps) and just brainstorm everything that you are. Write it down. Remember these are your deep intangible beliefs, not your tangible or physical attributes, but your thoughts and emotions that you believe. Be true to yourself and don't bullshit, and it will be an eye opening experience.

By doing this exercise you will not miraculously discover 'Who you are' but it will shine a light into the dark areas of your being and bring out all those beliefs that you are completely unconscious of, that rule the way you act and react every day.

And so, in this modern day and age, this is what your Fight or Flight response is reacting to. Whenever any of these deep intangible beliefs that make up the person we believe we are, are challenged or attacked, our body chemistry has the same response as a vulnerable animal in the jungle, it is an attack on our person and we need to either fight or run for the hills. This is anxiety.

So understand your reactions and stress about your financial status. Our bodies are still that of simple animals with hard wired systems that manifest as anxiety and stress when our perception of who we are is threatened, or when we believe we are not achieving the financial status we should be. Understand that we are constantly bombarded, via media in all its forms, with images and stories of who we should be. We believe that if we don't have the financial status of others then we are lower in the 'Food Chain', and therefore our chances of survival in the wild have dropped. We unconsciously strive to be the King of The Jungle as then we are not threatened.

What Influence do you have over your circumstances?

It's easy to blame other people, situations and circumstances for our financial place in the world, and it doesn't matter how comfortable we are, as humans we all want more, as the more we have the safer we will be when things get tough (see the survival neurons kicking in again?).

But what does blaming achieve? Really how much control do you have over the situations in your life?

Everyone knows the theory of the 'Butterfly Effect'.........ok if you don't you definitely should. We touched on this in **MIND – The Sixth Step on the Journey – The Myth of Control**. The term Butterfly Effect stems from the understanding of Chaos Theory stating that outcomes and results stem from dependence on initial conditions. The mathematician Edward Lorenz demonstrated that a small event leads to multiple actions and reactions and to many future events, but that a very small change in the conditions of the original event will dramatically change the outcomes of future events.

The simplest example is throwing dice. Every time you throw the dice, no matter how hard you try the conditions can never be repeated. The way the dice are held in the hand. The force they are thrown with. The angle of the throw. The state of the surface on which they are thrown. Etc. etc. It means that it is impossible to control the outcome of the dice in this event.

The name the 'Butterfly Effect' suggests that the simple flapping of a butterfly's wings on one side of the earth creates a hurricane on the other a few weeks later.

So imagine if human choice is added into the equation how complex events in our world become and hence you begin to understand Chaos Theory.

So Status Anxiety is the feeling of inadequacy, of not having enough wealth or 'toys' and that without that status you will not be taken seriously by the people who matter. It's a modern day disease that is perpetuated by our consumerist society where more is better.

TASK:

Think about where you see yourself in society. Where do you think you fit in? Who do you think is 'above' you or better than you? Why do you believe that? Often it's because they have more money or are perceived to be successful.

Really take apart the reasons you have put yourself at a certain level of status in your community. Understand that regardless of your wealth or your 'success' or your position, it makes you no better or worse than those above or below you.

Living
The Eleventh Step on the Journey....

Relationships

Our relationships with others, whilst they should never dictate who we are as a person, are critical to our enjoyment of life. Humans are naturally social creatures and the need for mutually beneficial relationships and companionship is essential to a happy life.

I'm very far from being a relationship guru and this is most definitely not a 'Dear Dorothy' answer to all your questions, but in my professional life as a Project Manager it is essential to understand that relationships with people is at the heart of what successful project management is all about. I started my project management career as one of the worst man-managers ever. I was constantly stressed, worried about the consequences of my actions, and more focused on not screwing up than on good outcomes.

> *What relationships are worth fighting for...and what ones should you just let go?*
>
> *JR*

My method of management was aggressive and forceful. It took me at least 10 years of heartache to start to realise that my methods were a complete waste of mine and everyone else's time. After this realisation it took me almost another 5 years to start to see real change in the way I conducted myself, the way I reacted to situations, and to become a conscious, proactive project manager. I've been a slow learner when it comes to relationships but having been a bad man manager, then becoming conscious of my shortcom-

ings, and working hard to understand how to improve, I feel I have a certain unique perspective on the subject.
When we talk relationships the immediate thinking is your relationship with your wife or partner, but relationships are significantly broader than that and to focus on one relationship at the expense of all others is a recipe for an unbalanced and unhappy life.

At the best of times Old Boys can find it hard to communicate emotions and feelings and the fear of looking weak is often a mask under which true feelings are kept and not expressed until it's too late. I'm certainly not talking about becoming an emotional cry baby who expresses his inner most feelings to anyone who will listen, but it's important we get a grip on ourselves, understand what relationships are worth fighting for, and how to have empathy and understanding for others.

Empathy and understanding of others is an absolutely essential element to relationship success. It doesn't matter if we are talking about a relationship with your wife, your work colleagues, your boss or your employees, we must try and understand the core issues that are causing the attitude of the other person. We've all heard the phrase 'Walk a mile in my shoes…' well that's what we need to do with our relationships. Remember that every person has their own perception of reality, their own version of what is right and what is wrong, and through all their past experiences they have built up certain beliefs and core values that dictate the way they look at the world. It doesn't make them right, but it also doesn't make them wrong, but either way it is real to them.

There is a technique in Life Coaching called Narrative Therapy (NT). The purpose of NT is to get the coachee to tell you their story, not the story of what they do for a living, but the story of why they are who they are. How do they view the world and their place in it and understand what past experiences and cultural influences have made them view the world in this way. The goal of NT is to identify Unique Outcomes which are times when things happened that contradicted their story, and how those Unique Outcomes came to be. This shows the coachee that the world is not necessarily exactly as they see it and that there are possible other ways things can happen, and other ways of interpreting experiences. By doing this it opens up the coachees mind to the way other people may see things and instead of simply seeing that other person as wrong, they may see a reason why the other person thinks that way, and that opens up a certain level of understanding and even empathy. From that position then a coachee can start to look at the world differently, to change the way they perceive events, and also to become more understanding of others views. With this better understanding of the way other people view the world you can then start to see the core issues affecting that person, and with that information you can start to answer their concerns and issues which will have a profound effect on the way they relate to you. This is an essential core of Relationship building.

There are many different relationships in our lives –

- Wife or partner
- Children
- Extended Family
- Work Colleagues
- Bosses

- Employees
- Friends and mates

Whilst every type of relationship is different the common core theme to the success of any relationship is being able to have a level of understanding of the other persons view, which when combined with a little empathy will allow you to see what the root issues are and to be able to start addressing them.

Of course you will never be able to develop a relationship with everyone and in your life there will be many more people than not who are diametrically opposed to your view that you simply cannot understand them, and there are always those people who are simply arseholes…..not much you can do about them. But this is where it is essential to have a clear understanding of what relationships are worth fighting for or at the very least are worth making an effort to try and understand the other persons view. Be very clear of the relationships you want to develop and make an effort to develop or save. The relationships that provide no value to your life…… just let them go. The problem is we often stress about the relationships that are not actually important to who we are, or to our goals, but just because these people have such a different world view then we feel the need to have to defend our views. You see this all over social media. Something happens or someone does something and all these people start commenting and making degrading comments and attacking the person. Why? They don't even know the person and it means absolutely nothing in the scheme of their own lives. People however feel the need to defend themselves against what is different, anything different to them is a potential attack on their own view of the world and the primal instinct kicks in and they must defend themselves.

Until you start to live consciously and acknowledge that others think differently to you, and that doesn't make them right or wrong, just different, you will be doomed to be continually stuck in the vortex of intolerance and your relationships will continue to flounder.

TASK:

Firstly list down all the relationships you have with people. List down not just the physical relationships, but also list down the relationships you have with people you don't know. I know that sounds a bit strange but as an example, at the time of writing this book Australia has a young talented Tennis player called Nick Kyrios who is making a complete tool of himself and is not endearing himself to the Australian public. It is amazing how mad people get about this, just have a quick look at social media. That is a relationship you have. Whilst you don't know the guy it impacts your life. So think hard about this, don't just write down the obvious, go right outside the box.

Now sort that list into 3 separate columns being –

1. Those relationships that make you happy or have the potential to make you happy

2. Those relationships that are important to your goals and aspirations

3. Those relationships that have no impact on your life goals other than emotional stress

Firstly dump every relationship in column 3. Stop following those people on Facebook, stop talking to them, stop any association you have. Move on!!

The relationships in column 1 are generally family and friends. These are important to your daily mental health and well-being. These are relationships that should be fostered and encouraged over the long term.

The relationships in column 2 are often work and career related and are important to your goals and aspirations in the shorter term.

Pick one relationship from each of columns 1 and 2. Now I want you to brainstorm in your journal a back story of that other person. I want you to identify the way that person views the world. Do they get stressed easily in certain situations? Do they react to certain situations in a way that is a problem for your relationship? I want you to write a fictional backstory and come up with reasons why that person is the way they are. There are no facts in this it is all made up. Imagine you have been given the responsibility of presenting this person to the world in a positive light and being able to show clearly why they think the way they do. Find excuses for them. Just make stuff up until you come up with a great story as to why they are an angry stressed person. You want a story that will make people feel empathy for them.

The point of this process is to see how many different ways there are of looking at the world. Everyone's life story is different and we simply don't know the full back stories of people and what has caused them to have the views and attitudes they do. There are so many variables in people's lives that we should never judge a book by its cover.

(**Foot Note**: Make sure you destroy this material when you have finished....you don't want that person finding a story written about them that involves a completely made up story......that may not be good for the relationship)

Living
The Twelfth Step on the Journey....

Food, Wine, Beer & Song

And so we come to this final step on the Journey and it's as straight forward as it gets............**get out and enjoy life.**

Open yourself up to new experiences. Enjoy the food and the wine, have the beer and dance to the songs that they say you're too old to dance to.

We all have our vices so enjoy them, just don't let them kill you.

I don't want to arrive in heaven with the body of an Adonis, having denied myself life's pleasures to reach the perfection of the human form. Nor do I want to be mourned for my passing.

No…I want to arrive in heaven at a rate of knots, sliding in sideways with a beer in one hand and chocolate in the other, while those left behind drink merrily, laugh, and wonder 'what the hell was he thinking?'

JR

Stop taking everything so seriously and just have some fun……………………It will all be over before you know it.

Clocks

He walks with a limp now,
There's pain in his hips,
He's old and frail,
All he can do is sit.

The kids they throw rocks,
At his house late at night,
He lives on his own,
The old man with his clocks.

They call him names,
Those kids down the street,
When he ventures outdoors,
Frail and weak.

And so he stays in,
Not afraid but resigned,
His life is a prison,
But not on the inside.

He sits and dreams of
Past glory and strife,
As the sun creeps slowly,
Across the living room of his life.

The curtains blow gently
The sun hits the floor,
And all he can hear are
The clocks on the wall.

Food, Wine, Beer & Song

He drifts off lightly
Into a world he knows well,
Where he's young and strong
And there's no living hell.

He remembers a wife,
Children on the shore,
Yet every day the clarity
Seems to fade more and more.

There's a CRACK on the window,
A stone thrown once more,
But in his stupor he dreams,
Is that the sound of war?

The years in trenches,
Knee deep in mud,
Surrounded by the dead,
Lying in blood.

He twitches and moans,
But he remains alone,
In the house of his childhood,
And once more his mind roams.

In the quiet of the night,
When the clocks are alive,
Oh the dreams you can have,
And the memories you can hide.

The 4 Pillars of Life

For this old man,
The clocks they speak,
Every tick, every tock,
They watch him grow weak.

And so the Old Man sits,
He listens to the chimes,
Of his life passing by,
And decides it's time.

So he closes his eyes,
Thanks god for his lot,
Breathes his last breath,
And all the clocks stop.

JR

www.ingramcontent.com/pod-product-compliance
Lightning Source LLC
Chambersburg PA
CBHW071855290426
44110CB00013B/1153